Nostalgic RECIPES From the

50's, 60's, 70's and 80's!

pi

Publications International, Ltd.

Art throughout and photograph on front cover (top right) copyright © Shutterstock.com.

Pictured on the front cover *(clockwise from top left):* Strawberry Salad *(page 44)*, Sloppy Joes *(page 90)*, Pineapple Upside Down Cake *(page 154)*, Meatloaf *(page 104)* and Black Forest Cake *(page 142)*.

Pictured on the back cover *(clockwise from top left):* Country Macaroni Salad *(page 34)*, Strawberry-Topped Pancakes *(page 64)*, Spicy Buttermilk Oven-Fried Chicken *(page 83)*, Lemon Meringue Pie *(page 170)* and Weeknight Chicken Tacos *(page 98)*.

ISBN: 978-1-63938-475-4

Manufactured in China.

8 7 6 5 4 3 2 1

Microwave Cooking: Microwave ovens vary in wattage. Use the cooking times as guidelines and check for doneness before adding more time.

Let's get social!

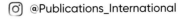 @Publications_International

 @PublicationsInternational

www.pilbooks.com

Contents

Snacks & Dips

Swell

Parmesan Ranch Snack Mix

Makes about 9½ cups

3 cups corn or rice cereal squares	2 tablespoons grated Parmesan cheese
2 cups oyster crackers	¼ cup (½ stick) butter, melted
1 package (5 ounces) bagel chips, broken in half	1 package (1 ounce) dry ranch salad dressing mix
1½ cups mini pretzel twists	½ teaspoon garlic powder
1 cup shelled pistachio nuts	

Slow Cooker Directions

1. Combine cereal, oyster crackers, bagel chips, pretzels, pistachios and cheese in slow cooker; mix gently.

2. Combine butter, salad dressing mix and garlic powder in small bowl. Pour over cereal mixture; toss lightly to coat. Cover; cook on LOW 3 hours.

3. Remove cover; stir gently. Cook, uncovered, on LOW 30 minutes.

5

Quick and Easy Stuffed Mushrooms

Makes 8 servings

1 **slice whole wheat bread**

16 **white or cremini mushrooms**

½ **cup sliced celery**

½ **cup chopped onion**

1 **clove garlic**

1 **teaspoon vegetable oil**

1 **teaspoon Worcestershire sauce**

½ **teaspoon dried marjoram**

⅛ **teaspoon ground red pepper**

Salt and black pepper

Dash paprika

1. Preheat oven to 350°F. Tear bread into pieces; place in food processor. Process 30 seconds or until crumbs are formed. Transfer to medium bowl.

2. Remove stems from mushrooms; reserve caps. Place mushroom stems, celery, onion and garlic in food processor; pulse until vegetables are finely chopped.

3. Heat oil in large skillet over medium heat. Add vegetable mixture; cook and stir 5 minutes or until onion is tender. Add to bread crumbs. Stir in Worcestershire sauce, marjoram and red pepper; season to taste with salt and pepper.

4. Fill mushroom caps evenly with mixture, pressing down firmly. Place about ½ inch apart in shallow baking pan. Spray tops with nonstick cooking spray. Sprinkle with paprika.

5. Bake 15 minutes or until heated through.

 Note Mushrooms can be stuffed up to 1 day ahead; cover and refrigerate until ready to serve. Bake in preheated 300°F oven 20 minutes or until heated through.

Texas Caviar

Makes about 9 cups

- 1 tablespoon vegetable oil
- 1 cup fresh corn (from 2 to 3 ears)
- 2 cans (about 15 ounces each) black-eyed peas, rinsed and drained
- 1 can (about 15 ounces) black beans, rinsed and drained
- 1 cup halved grape tomatoes
- 1 bell pepper (red, orange, yellow or green), finely chopped
- ½ cup finely chopped red onion

- 1 jalapeño pepper, seeded and minced
- 2 green onions, minced
- ¼ cup chopped fresh cilantro
- 2 tablespoons red wine vinegar
- 1 tablespoon plus 1 teaspoon lime juice, divided
- 1 teaspoon salt
- 1 teaspoon sugar
- ½ teaspoon ground cumin
- ½ teaspoon dried oregano
- 2 cloves garlic, minced
- ¼ cup olive oil

1. Heat vegetable oil in large skillet over high heat. Add corn; cook and stir about 3 minutes or until corn is beginning to brown in spots. Place in large bowl. Add beans, tomatoes, bell pepper, onion, jalapeño, green onions and cilantro.

2. Combine vinegar, 1 tablespoon lime juice, salt, sugar, cumin, oregano and garlic in small bowl. Whisk in olive oil in thin steady stream until well blended. Pour over vegetables; stir to coat.

3. Refrigerate at least 2 hours or overnight. Just before serving, stir in remaining 1 teaspoon lime juice. Taste and season with additional salt, if desired.

Nutty Bacon Cheese Ball

Makes about 24 servings

1 package (8 ounces) cream cheese, softened

1/2 cup milk

2 cups (8 ounces) shredded sharp Cheddar cheese

2 cups (8 ounces) shredded Monterey Jack cheese

1/4 cup crumbled blue cheese

10 slices bacon, cooked, crumbled and divided

3/4 cup finely chopped pecans, toasted,* divided

1/4 cup finely minced green onions (white parts only)

1 jar (2 ounces) diced pimiento, drained

Salt and black pepper

1/4 cup minced fresh parsley

1 tablespoon poppy seeds

*To toast pecans, spread in single layer in small heavy skillet. Cook over medium heat 1 to 2 minutes or until lightly browned, stirring frequently. Remove from skillet; cool before using.

1. Beat cream cheese and milk in large bowl with electric mixer at low speed until blended. Add cheeses; beat at medium speed until well mixed. Add half of bacon, half of pecans, green onions and pimiento; beat until blended. Season with salt and pepper to taste. Transfer half of mixture to large piece of plastic wrap. Shape into ball; wrap tightly. Repeat with remaining mixture. Refrigerate at least 2 hours or until chilled.

2. Combine remaining bacon, pecans, parsley and poppy seeds in shallow bowl. Remove plastic wrap from chilled cheese balls. Roll each in bacon mixture until well coated. Wrap balls tightly in plastic wrap; refrigerate up to 24 hours.

Creamy Cheesy Spinach Dip

Makes about 4 cups

2 packages (10 ounces each) frozen chopped spinach, thawed

2 cups chopped onions

1 teaspoon salt

½ teaspoon garlic powder

¼ teaspoon black pepper

12 ounces pepper jack-flavored pasteurized process cheese product, cubed

Crackers and cut-up vegetables

Slow Cooker Directions

1. Drain spinach and squeeze dry, reserving ¾ cup liquid. Combine spinach, reserved liquid, onions, salt, garlic powder and black pepper in 1½-quart slow cooker; mix well. Cover; cook on HIGH 1½ hours.

2. Stir in cheese product; cook 30 minutes or until melted. Serve with crackers and vegetables.

 Tip To thaw spinach quickly, remove paper wrapper from spinach containers. Microwave on HIGH 3 to 4 minutes or until just thawed.

Classic Deviled Eggs

Makes 12 deviled eggs

6 eggs

3 tablespoons mayonnaise

½ teaspoon cider vinegar

½ teaspoon yellow mustard

⅛ teaspoon salt

Optional toppings: black pepper, paprika, minced fresh chives and/ or minced red onion (optional)

1. Bring medium saucepan of water to a boil. Gently add eggs with slotted spoon. Reduce heat to maintain a simmer; cook 12 minutes. Meanwhile, fill medium bowl with cold water and ice cubes. Drain eggs and place in ice water; cool 10 minutes.

2. Carefully peel eggs. Cut eggs in half; place yolks in small bowl. Add mayonnaise, vinegar, mustard and salt; mash until well blended. Spoon mixture into egg whites; garnish with desired toppings.

Buffalo Wings

Makes 4 servings

1 cup hot pepper sauce

⅓ cup vegetable oil, plus additional for frying

1 teaspoon sugar

½ teaspoon ground red pepper

½ teaspoon garlic powder

½ teaspoon Worcestershire sauce

⅛ teaspoon black pepper

1 pound chicken wings, tips discarded, separated at joints

Blue cheese dressing, store-bought or homemade (page 58)

Celery sticks

1. Combine hot pepper sauce, ⅓ cup oil, sugar, red pepper, garlic powder, Worcestershire sauce and black pepper in small saucepan; cook over medium heat 20 minutes. Place large wire rack over paper towels. Pour sauce into large bowl.

2. Heat 3 inches of oil in large saucepan over medium-high heat to 350°F; adjust heat to maintain temperature during frying. Add wings; cook 10 minutes or until crispy. Drain on prepared wire rack.

3. Remove wings to bowl of sauce; toss to coat. Serve with blue cheese dressing and celery sticks.

Seven-Layer Dip

Makes 10 servings

1 package (3 ounces) ramen noodles, crushed*

2 tablespoons taco seasoning mix

3 ripe avocados, diced

1 jalapeño pepper, finely chopped

2 tablespoons finely chopped fresh cilantro

2 tablespoons lime juice

1 clove garlic, minced

½ teaspoon salt

1 can (about 15 ounces) refried beans

1 container (16 ounces) sour cream

2 cups (8 ounces) shredded Cheddar-Jack cheese or Mexican cheese blend

2 medium tomatoes, diced

3 green onions, thinly sliced

Tortilla chips

*Use any flavor; discard seasoning packet.

1. Combine noodles and taco seasoning mix in medium bowl; mix well.

2. Mash avocados, jalapeño, cilantro, lime juice, garlic and salt in large bowl until well blended.

3. Spread refried beans in bottom of 8-inch glass bowl or baking dish. Layer sour cream, noodles, avocado mixture, cheese, tomatoes and green onions evenly over beans. Serve immediately or cover and refrigerate for up to 8 hours. Serve with tortilla chips.

Sweet and Tangy Meatballs

Makes about 4 dozen meatballs

2 **pounds ground beef**	1/2 **teaspoon black pepper**
1 1/3 **cups ketchup, divided**	1 **cup packed brown sugar**
1 **egg, lightly beaten**	1 **can (6 ounces) tomato paste**
3 **tablespoons seasoned dry bread crumbs**	1/4 **cup soy sauce**
2 **tablespoons dried onion flakes**	1/4 **cup cider vinegar**
3/4 **teaspoon garlic salt**	1 1/2 **teaspoons hot pepper sauce**

Slow Cooker Directions

1. Preheat oven to 350°F. Combine beef, 1/3 cup ketchup, egg, bread crumbs, onion flakes, garlic salt and black pepper in large bowl. Mix lightly but thoroughly; shape into 1-inch meatballs.

2. Arrange meatballs in single layer on two 15×10-inch jelly-roll pans. Bake 18 minutes or until browned. Transfer meatballs to slow cooker.

3. Combine remaining 1 cup ketchup, brown sugar, tomato paste, soy sauce, vinegar and hot pepper sauce in medium bowl. Pour over meatballs. Cover; cook on LOW 4 hours. Serve with cocktail picks.

Cheesy Fondue

Makes 4 servings

2 cups (8 ounces) shredded Swiss cheese

2 cups (8 ounces) shredded Monterey Jack cheese

2 tablespoons all-purpose flour

1½ cups dry white wine or apple juice

Dash ground nutmeg

Dash ground red pepper

French bread cubes and sliced Granny Smith apple

1. Combine cheeses and flour in large bowl; toss lightly to coat.

2. Bring wine to a simmer over medium heat in fondue pot. Gradually add cheese mixture until melted, stirring constantly. Stir in nutmeg and pepper. Serve with bread cubes and apple for dipping. Keep warm, stirring occasionally.

Spicy BBQ Party Franks

Makes 6 to 8 servings

1 **package (16 ounces) cocktail franks**	2 **tablespoons packed dark brown sugar**
1 **tablespoon butter**	2 **tablespoons hot pepper sauce**
1/3 **cup cola**	1 **tablespoon cider vinegar**
1/3 **cup ketchup**	

1. Pierce cocktail franks with fork. Melt butter in large skillet over medium heat. Add franks; cook until lightly browned.

2. Stir in cola, ketchup, brown sugar, hot pepper sauce and vinegar. Reduce heat to low; cook until sauce is reduced to sticky glaze.

Veggie Appetizer Pizza

Makes 2 dozen squares

2 packages (8 ounces each) refrigerated crescent roll dough

12 ounces cream cheese, softened

1 cup sour cream

2 tablespoons dry ranch salad dressing mix (about $1/2$ package)

$3/4$ cup cucumber slices

2 cups broccoli florets

$1/2$ cup carrots slices

$3/4$ cup grape tomatoes, cut in half

1. Preheat oven to 375°F. Place dough in single layer in ungreased 15×10-inch baking sheet. Press onto bottom and up sides of pan, sealing perforations. Bake 13 to 17 minutes or until brown. Cool on wire rack at least 30 minutes.

2. Beat cream cheese in medium bowl with electric mixer at medium speed until fluffy. Add sour cream and salad dressing mix; beat until blended. Spread over cooled crust.

3. Cut cucumber slices in half. Arrange cucumber slices, broccoli florets, carrot slices and tomato halves on pizza. Cut pizza into squares; serve immediately or cover and refrigerate for up to 24 hours.

Bacon-Wrapped Teriyaki Shrimp

Makes 4 to 5 servings

1 pound large raw shrimp, peeled and deveined (with tails on)

¼ cup teriyaki marinade

11 to 12 slices bacon, cut in half crosswise

1. Preheat oven to 425°F. Line shallow baking pan with foil.

2. Place shrimp in large resealable food storage bag. Add teriyaki marinade; seal bag and turn to coat. Marinate in refrigerator 15 to 20 minutes.

3. Remove shrimp from bag; reserve marinade. Wrap each shrimp with one piece of bacon. Place shrimp in prepared baking pan; brush bacon with some of reserved marinade.

4. Bake 15 minutes or until bacon is crisp and shrimp are pink and opaque.

 Tip Do not use thick-cut bacon for this recipe, because the bacon will not be completely cooked when the shrimp are cooked through.

Spinach-Artichoke Dip

Makes 6 to 8 servings

1 package (8 ounces) baby spinach

1 package (8 ounces) cream cheese, softened

¼ cup mayonnaise

1 clove garlic, minced

1 teaspoon dried basil

½ teaspoon dried thyme

¼ teaspoon salt

¼ teaspoon red pepper flakes

¼ teaspoon black pepper

1 can (about 14 ounces) artichoke hearts, drained and chopped

¾ cup grated Parmesan cheese, divided

Toasted French bread slices or tortilla chips

1. Preheat oven to 350°F. Spray 8-inch oval, round or square baking dish with nonstick cooking spray.

2. Place spinach in large microwavable bowl; cover and microwave on HIGH 2 minutes or until wilted. Uncover; let stand until cool enough to handle. Squeeze dry and coarsely chop.

3. Whisk cream cheese, mayonnaise, garlic, basil, thyme, salt, red pepper flakes and black pepper in medium bowl until well blended. Stir in spinach, artichokes and ½ cup Parmesan. Spread in prepared baking dish; sprinkle with remaining ¼ cup Parmesan.

4. Bake about 30 minutes or until edges are golden brown. Cool slightly; serve warm with toasted bread slices.

Nifty Soups & Salads

Cranberry Crunch Gelatin Salad

Makes 8 servings

2 cups boiling water

2 packages (4-serving size each) cherry-flavored gelatin

1 can (16 ounces) whole berry cranberry sauce

1½ cups mini marshmallows

1 cup coarsely chopped walnuts

1. Stir boiling water into gelatin in large bowl 2 minutes or until completely dissolved. Chill 2 hours or until slightly set.

2. Fold cranberry sauce, marshmallows and walnuts into gelatin mixture. Pour into 6-cup gelatin mold. Cover; refrigerate at least 4 hours or until set. Remove from mold.

Country Macaroni Salad

Makes 6 servings

- 1 cup uncooked elbow macaroni
- 6 tablespoons mayonnaise
- 1/4 cup plain yogurt or sour cream
- 1 tablespoon sweet pickle relish
- 1 teaspoon dried dill weed
- 1 teaspoon yellow mustard
- 1/2 teaspoon salt
- 1 cup thawed frozen peas
- 1 cup chopped green bell pepper
- 1/2 cup thinly sliced celery
- 8 ounces ham, cubed
- 1/2 cup (2 ounces) shredded Cheddar cheese, divided

1. Cook pasta in large saucepan of salted boiling water according to package directions until tender. Drain and rinse under cold water until completely cooled.

2. Meanwhile, combine mayonnaise, yogurt, relish, dill weed, mustard and salt in large bowl; stir until well blended. Add pasta, peas, bell pepper, celery and ham; mix well.

3. Stir in 1/4 cup cheese; toss lightly. Sprinkle with remaining 1/4 cup cheese. Serve immediately or refrigerate until ready to serve.

Favorite Beef Stew

Makes 6 servings

3 carrots, halved and cut into 1-inch pieces

3 stalks celery, cut into 1-inch pieces

2 large potatoes, peeled and cut into ½-inch pieces

2 tablespoons Worcestershire sauce

1 bay leaf

2 teaspoons salt, divided

¾ teaspoon dried thyme

¾ teaspoon dried basil

1 can (about 14 ounces) diced tomatoes

2 pounds beef stew meat (1-inch pieces)

¼ cup all-purpose flour

½ teaspoon black pepper

2 tablespoons vegetable oil

1½ cups chopped onions

3 cloves garlic, chopped

1 can (about 14 ounces) beef broth

Slow Cooker Directions

1. Layer carrots, celery, potatoes, Worcestershire sauce and bay leaf in slow cooker. Sprinkle with 1 teaspoon salt, thyme and basil. Pour tomatoes over vegetables.

2. Toss beef, flour, remaining 1 teaspoon salt and pepper in large bowl until beef is coated. Heat oil in large skillet over medium-high heat. Cook beef in batches about 10 minutes or until browned on all sides. Transfer beef to slow cooker. Add onions and garlic to same skillet; cook and stir over medium-high heat 5 minutes or until onion is softened. Add broth, stirring to scrape up browned bits. Pour onion mixture into slow cooker.

3. Cover; cook on LOW 8 to 9 hours or until beef is very tender.

Lime & Pineapple Seafoam Salad

Makes 8 to 10 servings

2 cans (8 ounces each) crushed pineapple in juice

1 package (4-serving size) lime gelatin

1 cup boiling water

1/2 cup cold water

1 package (8 ounces) cream cheese, softened

3/4 cup coarsely chopped pecans

2/3 cup celery slices

1 1/2 cups thawed whipped topping

1. Drain pineapple in sieve set over medium bowl. Squeeze pineapple to remove most of juice; reserve 3 tablespoons juice.

2. Place gelatin in medium bowl; stir in boiling water until gelatin is dissolved. Stir in cold water and reserved 3 tablespoons pineapple juice.

3. Beat cream cheese in large bowl with electric mixer until smooth. Beat in 1/4 cup gelatin mixture until blended. Slowly beat in remaining gelatin mixture. Cover and refrigerate 1 hour or until thickened.

4. Stir in pineapple, pecans and celery. Fold in whipped topping. Pour into serving bowl. Chill 2 hours or until set.

New England Clam Chowder

Makes 4 servings

2 cans (5 ounces each) whole baby clams, undrained

2 baking potatoes, peeled and coarsely chopped

$\frac{1}{2}$ cup finely chopped onion

$1\frac{1}{3}$ cups evaporated milk

$\frac{1}{2}$ teaspoon white pepper

$\frac{1}{2}$ teaspoon dried thyme

2 tablespoons butter

Salt and additional white pepper

1. Drain clams, reserving juice. Add enough water to reserved juice to measure $1\frac{1}{3}$ cups. Combine clam juice mixture, potato and onion in medium saucepan; bring to a boil over high heat. Reduce heat to low; simmer 8 minutes or until potato is tender.

2. Add evaporated milk, $\frac{1}{2}$ teaspoon pepper and thyme to saucepan; cook and stir 2 minutes over medium-high heat. Add butter; cook 5 minutes or until soup thickens, stirring occasionally.

3. Add clams; cook 5 minutes or until clams are firm, stirring occasionally. Season to taste with salt and additional pepper.

Italian Salad

Makes 4 servings

Dressing

- ½ cup mayonnaise
- ½ cup white wine vinegar
- ¼ cup grated Parmesan cheese
- 1 tablespoon olive oil
- 1 tablespoon lemon juice
- 1 tablespoon corn syrup
- 1 clove garlic, minced
- ¾ teaspoon Italian seasoning
- ½ teaspoon salt
- ½ teaspoon black pepper

Salad

- 1 package (10 ounces) Italian salad blend
- 2 plum tomatoes, thinly sliced
- 1 cup croutons
- ½ cup thinly sliced red or green bell pepper
- ½ cup thinly sliced red onion
- ¼ cup sliced black olives

  Pepperoncini peppers (optional)

1. For dressing, whisk mayonnaise, vinegar, cheese, oil, lemon juice, corn syrup, garlic, Italian seasoning, salt and black pepper in medium bowl until well blended.

2. For salad, place salad blend in large bowl; top with tomatoes, croutons, bell pepper, onion and olives. Add dressing; toss to coat. Top with pepperoncini, if desired.

Strawberry Salad

Makes 12 to 14 servings

2 packages (4-serving size each) strawberry-flavored gelatin

1 cup boiling water

2 packages (10 ounces each) frozen strawberries, thawed

1 can (20 ounces) crushed pineapple, drained

2 cups sour cream

1 container (8 ounces) thawed whipped topping

Sliced fresh strawberries and fresh mint leaves (optional)

1. Combine gelatin and boiling water in large bowl; stir until dissolved. Add frozen strawberries and pineapple; mix well.

2. Pour half of gelatin mixture into medium glass serving bowl or 13×9-inch baking dish. Refrigerate until soft set.

3. Spread sour cream over gelatin in bowl. Pour remaining gelatin mixture over sour cream. Refrigerate until ready to serve. Spread whipped topping over gelatin; garnish with fresh strawberries and mint.

Deli Chicken Noodle Soup

Makes 8 servings (10 cups)

2 tablespoons butter	4 cups chicken broth, divided
1 cup chopped onion	2 cups water
1 cup sliced carrots	1 tablespoon minced fresh parsley
½ cup diced celery	1½ teaspoons salt
2 tablespoons vegetable oil	½ teaspoon black pepper
1 pound chicken breast tenderloins	3 cups uncooked egg noodles
1 pound chicken thigh fillets	

1. Melt butter in large saucepan or Dutch oven over medium-low heat. Add onion, carrots and celery; cook 8 minutes or until vegetables are soft, stirring occasionally.

2. Meanwhile, heat oil in large skillet over medium-high heat. Add chicken in single layer; cook 12 minutes or until lightly browned and cooked through, turning once. Remove chicken to large cutting board. Add 1 cup broth to skillet; cook 1 minute, scraping up browned bits from bottom of skillet. Add broth to vegetables in saucepan. Stir in remaining 3 cups broth, water, 1 tablespoon parsley, salt and pepper.

3. Chop chicken into 1-inch pieces when cool enough to handle. Add to soup; bring to a boil over medium-high heat. Reduce heat to medium-low; cook 15 minutes. Add noodles; cook 15 minutes or until noodles are tender.

Tex-Mex Style Chili

Makes 4 servings

1 **pound ground beef**

¾ **cup chopped onion**

½ **teaspoon black pepper**

¼ **teaspoon salt**

2 **cans (about 14 ounces each) diced tomatoes with green chiles, undrained**

1 **can (15 ounces) chili beans in sauce**

1 **cup water**

1 **package (1¼ ounces) chili seasoning mix**

2 **cups (8 ounces) shredded Cheddar cheese**

1. Brown beef in large skillet over medium-high heat 6 to 8 minutes, stirring to break up meat. Drain fat. Add onion, pepper and salt; cook and stir until onion is tender.

2. Stir in tomatoes with juice, beans with sauce, water and seasoning mix; simmer 25 minutes, stirring occasionally. Ladle into bowls; sprinkle with cheese.

Cheesy Waldorf Salad

Makes 6 to 8 servings

⅓ cup mayonnaise

1 tablespoon honey

1 tablespoon cider vinegar

4 small *or* 3 large apples,
cored and cut into ½-inch
pieces (about 4 cups)

4 ounces provolone cheese,
cubed

2 stalks celery, thinly sliced

½ cup chopped walnuts or
pecans, toasted,* divided

Red leaf lettuce leaves

*To toast walnuts, spread in single layer
in small heavy skillet. Cook over medium
heat 1 to 2 minutes or until lightly browned,
stirring frequently. Remove from skillet; cool
before using.

1. Combine mayonnaise, honey and vinegar in large bowl until blended. Add apples, cheese, celery and ¼ cup walnuts; stir to coat. (At this point salad may be refrigerated up to 8 hours.)

2. To serve, line individual salad plates with lettuce; top with salad. Sprinkle remaining ¼ cup walnuts over each serving.

 Tip Substitute cubed cooked chicken for the cheese for a more traditional Waldorf salad.

Broccoli Cheese Soup

Makes 4 to 6 servings

6 tablespoons (³/₄ stick) butter

1 cup chopped onion

1 clove garlic, minced

¹/₄ cup all-purpose flour

2 cups vegetable broth

2 cups milk

1¹/₂ teaspoons Dijon mustard

¹/₂ teaspoon salt

¹/₄ teaspoon ground nutmeg

¹/₄ teaspoon black pepper

¹/₈ teaspoon hot pepper sauce

1 package (16 ounces) frozen broccoli (5 cups)

2 carrots, shredded (1 cup)

6 ounces pasteurized process cheese product, cubed

1 cup (4 ounces) shredded sharp Cheddar cheese, plus additional for garnish

1. Melt butter in large saucepan or Dutch oven over medium-low heat. Add onion; cook and stir 8 minutes or until softened. Add garlic; cook and stir 1 minute. Increase heat to medium. Whisk in flour until smooth; cook and stir 3 minutes without browning.

2. Gradually whisk in broth and milk. Add mustard, salt, nutmeg, black pepper and hot pepper sauce; cook 15 minutes or until thickened, stirring occasionally.

3. Add broccoli; cook 15 minutes. Add carrots; cook 10 minutes or until vegetables are tender.

4. Remove half of soup to food processor or blender; process until smooth. Return to saucepan. Add cheese product and 1 cup Cheddar; cook and stir over low heat until cheese is melted. Ladle soup into bowls; garnish with additional Cheddar.

Wedge Salad

Makes 4 servings

Dressing

- ³/₄ cup mayonnaise
- ½ cup buttermilk
- 1 cup crumbled blue cheese, divided
- 1 clove garlic, minced
- ½ teaspoon sugar
- ⅛ teaspoon onion powder
- ⅛ teaspoon salt
- ⅛ teaspoon black pepper

Salad

- 1 head iceberg lettuce
- 1 large tomato, diced (about 1 cup)
- ½ small red onion, cut into thin rings
- ½ cup crumbled crisp-cooked bacon (6 to 8 slices)

1. For dressing, combine mayonnaise, buttermilk, ½ cup cheese, garlic, sugar, onion powder, salt and pepper in food processor or blender; process until smooth.

2. For salad, cut lettuce into quarters through stem end; remove stem from each wedge. Place wedges on individual serving plates; top with dressing. Sprinkle with tomato, onion, remaining ½ cup cheese and bacon.

Creamy Tomato Soup

Makes 4 to 6 servings

3 tablespoons olive oil, divided

2 tablespoons butter

1 large onion, finely chopped

2 cloves garlic, minced

2 teaspoons sugar

1 teaspoon salt

1/2 teaspoon dried oregano

2 cans (28 ounces each) whole tomatoes, undrained

4 cups 1/2-inch focaccia cubes (half of 9-ounce loaf)

1/2 teaspoon freshly ground black pepper

1/2 cup whipping cream

1. Heat 2 tablespoons oil and butter in large saucepan or Dutch oven over medium-high heat. Add onion; cook and stir 5 minutes or until softened. Add garlic, sugar, salt and oregano; cook and stir 30 seconds. Stir in tomatoes with juice; bring to a boil. Reduce heat to medium-low; simmer 45 minutes, stirring occasionally.

2. Meanwhile, prepare croutons. Preheat oven to 350°F. Combine focaccia cubes, remaining 1 tablespoon oil and pepper in large bowl; toss to coat. Spread on large rimmed baking sheet. Bake 10 minutes or until bread cubes are golden brown.

3. Blend soup with immersion blender until smooth. (Or process soup in batches in food processor or blender.) Stir in cream; cook until heated through. Ladle soup into bowls; top with croutons.

Cobb Salad

Makes 4 servings

1 package (10 ounces) torn
   mixed salad greens *or*
   8 cups torn romaine
   lettuce

6 ounces cooked chicken, cut
   into bite-size pieces

1 tomato, seeded and
   chopped

2 hard-cooked eggs, cut into
   bite-size pieces

4 slices bacon, crisp-cooked
   and crumbled

1 avocado, diced

1 large carrot, shredded

1/2 cup blue cheese, crumbled

Blue cheese dressing,
   prepared or homemade
   (recipe follows)

1. Place lettuce in serving bowl. Arrange chicken, tomato, eggs, bacon, avocado, carrot and cheese in rows on top of lettuce.

2. Serve with dressing.

Blue Cheese Dressing: Combine 3/4 cup mayonnaise, 1/2 cup buttermilk, 1/2 cup crumbled blue cheese, 1 clove garlic, minced, 1/2 teaspoon sugar, 1/8 teaspoon salt and 1/8 teaspoon black pepper in food processor or blender; process until smooth.

Balsamic Green Bean Almondine

Makes 4 servings

1 **pound fresh green beans, trimmed**

2 **teaspoons olive oil**

2 **teaspoons balsamic vinegar**

1/2 **teaspoon salt**

1/4 **teaspoon black pepper**

2 **tablespoons sliced almonds, toasted***

*To toast almonds, spread in single layer in small heavy skillet. Cook over medium heat 1 to 2 minutes or until lightly browned, stirring frequently. Remove from skillet; cool before using.

1. Place beans in medium saucepan; cover with water. Bring to a simmer over high heat. Reduce heat; simmer, uncovered, 4 to 8 minutes or until beans are crisp-tender. Drain well and return to saucepan.

2. Add oil, vinegar, salt and pepper; toss to coat. Sprinkle with almonds.

Diner & Deli
Delights

The Great Reuben Sandwich

Makes 2 sandwiches

4 slices rye bread

¼ cup Thousand Island dressing (see Tip)

8 ounces thinly sliced corned beef or pastrami

4 slices (1 ounce each) Swiss cheese

½ cup sauerkraut, well drained

2 tablespoons butter

1. Spread one side of each bread slice with dressing. Layer with corned beef, cheese, sauerkraut and remaining bread slices.

2. Melt butter in large skillet over medium heat. Add sandwiches; press down with spatula or weigh down with small plate. Cook sandwiches 6 minutes per side or until cheese is melted and bread is lightly browned. Serve immediately.

 Tip For a quick homemade Thousand Island dressing, combine 2 tablespoons mayonnaise, 2 tablespoons sweet pickle relish and 1 tablespoon cocktail sauce in small bowl.

Strawberry-Topped Pancakes

Makes 2 servings (6 large pancakes)

1½ cups sliced fresh
    strawberries

2 tablespoons seedless
    strawberry jam

1¼ cups all-purpose flour

¼ cup sugar

1 teaspoon baking powder

1 teaspoon baking soda

¼ teaspoon salt

1¼ cups buttermilk

1 egg, lightly beaten

1 to 2 tablespoons vegetable
    oil

Whipped cream (optional)

1. Combine strawberries and strawberry jam in medium bowl; stir gently to coat. Set aside.

2. Combine flour, sugar, baking powder, baking soda and salt in large bowl; mix well. Add buttermilk and egg; whisk until blended.

3. Heat 1 tablespoon oil in large skillet over medium heat or brush griddle with oil. For each pancake, pour ½ cup batter into skillet, spreading into 5- to 6-inch circle. Cook 3 to 4 minutes or until bottom is golden brown and small bubbles appear on surface. Turn pancake; cook 2 minutes or until golden brown. Repeat with remaining batter, adding additional oil as needed.

4. For each serving, stack three pancakes; top with strawberry mixture and garnish with whipped cream.

Joe's Special

Makes 4 to 6 servings

1 tablespoon vegetable oil	1/2 teaspoon garlic powder
1 pound ground beef	1/2 teaspoon salt
2 cups sliced mushrooms	1 package (10 ounces) frozen chopped spinach, thawed
1 small onion, chopped	4 eggs, lightly beaten
2 teaspoons Worcestershire sauce	1/3 cup grated Parmesan cheese
1 teaspoon dried oregano	
1 teaspoon ground nutmeg	

1. Heat oil in large skillet over medium-high heat. Add ground beef, mushrooms and onion; cook and stir 6 to 8 minutes or until beef is no longer pink, stirring to break up meat. Add Worcestershire sauce, oregano, nutmeg, garlic powder and salt.

2. Drain spinach (do not squeeze dry); stir into meat mixture. Push mixture to one side of pan. Reduce heat to medium. Pour eggs into other side of pan; cook without stirring 1 to 2 minutes or until set on bottom. Lift eggs to allow uncooked portion to flow underneath. Repeat until softly set. Gently stir into meat mixture; cook until heated through. Stir in cheese.

Tuna Salad Sandwich

Makes 2 servings

1 can (12 ounces) solid white albacore tuna, drained

1 can (5 ounces) chunk white albacore tuna, drained

¼ cup mayonnaise

1 tablespoon pickle relish

2 teaspoons spicy brown mustard

1 teaspoon lemon juice

½ teaspoon salt

¼ teaspoon black pepper

French bread or focaccia (about 4×3 inch pieces), split and toasted or 4 slices honey wheat bread

Lettuce, tomato and red onion slices

1. Place tuna in medium bowl; flake with fork. Add mayonnaise, pickle relish, mustard, lemon juice, salt and pepper; mix well.

2. Serve tuna salad on focaccia with lettuce, tomato and onion.

Corned Beef Hash

Makes 4 servings

2 large russet potatoes, peeled and cut into 1/2-inch cubes	1 cup chopped onion
1/2 teaspoon salt	8 ounces corned beef, finely chopped
1/4 teaspoon black pepper	1 tablespoon horseradish
1/4 cup (1/2 stick) butter	4 eggs

1. Place potatoes in large skillet; add water to cover. Bring to a boil over high heat. Reduce heat to low; simmer 6 minutes. (Potatoes will be firm.) Drain potatoes; place in medium bowl. Sprinkle with salt and pepper.

2. Melt butter in same skillet over medium heat. Add onion; cook and stir 5 minutes or until softened. Add corned beef, horseradish and potatoes; mix well. Press mixture with spatula to flatten.

3. Reduce heat to low; cook 10 to 15 minutes. Turn hash in large pieces; pat down and cook 10 to 15 minutes or until bottom is well browned.

4. Meanwhile, bring 1 inch of water to a simmer in small saucepan. Break 1 egg into shallow dish; carefully slide into water. Cook 5 minutes or until white is opaque. Remove with slotted spoon to plate; keep warm. Repeat with remaining eggs.

5. Top each serving of hash with one egg. Serve immediately.

Classic Patty Melts

Makes 4 servings

5	tablespoons butter, divided	¹/₂	teaspoon onion powder
2	large yellow onions, thinly sliced	¹/₄	teaspoon black pepper
³/₄	teaspoon plus pinch of salt, divided	8	slices marble rye bread
1	pound ground chuck (80% lean)	¹/₂	cup Thousand Island dressing
¹/₂	teaspoon garlic powder	8	slices (about 1 ounce each) deli American or Swiss cheese

1. Melt 2 tablespoons butter in large skillet over medium heat. Add onions and pinch of salt; cook 20 minutes or until onions are very soft and golden brown, stirring occasionally. Remove to small bowl; wipe out skillet with paper towel.

2. Combine beef, remaining ³/₄ teaspoon salt, garlic powder, onion powder and pepper in medium bowl; mix gently. Shape into four patties about the size and shape of bread slices and ¹/₄ to ¹/₂ inch thick.

3. Melt 1 tablespoon butter in same skillet over medium-high heat. Add two patties at a time 3 minutes or until bottoms are browned, pressing down gently with spatula to form crust. Turn patties; cook 3 minutes or until browned. Remove patties to plate; wipe out skillet with paper towel.

4. Spread one side of each bread slice with dressing. Top four bread slices with cheese slice, patty, caramelized onions, another cheese slice and remaining bread slices.

5. Melt 1 tablespoon butter in same skillet over medium heat. Add two sandwiches to skillet; cook 4 minutes or until golden brown, pressing down with spatula to crisp bread. Turn sandwiches; cook 4 minutes or until golden brown and cheese is melted. Repeat with remaining 1 tablespoon butter and sandwiches.

Spinach Quiche

1 **medium leek**

¼ **cup (½ stick) butter**

2 **cups finely chopped cooked chicken**

½ **package (10 ounces) frozen chopped spinach or broccoli, cooked and drained**

1 **unbaked ready-to-use pie crust (10 inches in diameter)***

1½ **cups (6 ounces) shredded Swiss cheese**

1 **tablespoon all-purpose flour**

1½ **cups half-and-half or evaporated milk**

4 **eggs**

2 **tablespoons brandy**

½ **teaspoon salt**

¼ **teaspoon black pepper**

¼ **teaspoon ground nutmeg**

*Use a frozen pie crust or one refrigerated pie crust (half of a 15-ounce package) pressed into a 10-inch pie plate.

1. Preheat oven to 375°F. Cut leek in half lengthwise; wash and trim, leaving 2 to 3 inches of green tops intact. Cut leek halves crosswise into thin slices. Place in small saucepan; add enough water to cover. Bring to a boil over high heat; reduce heat and simmer 5 minutes. Drain and set aside.

2. Melt butter in large skillet over medium heat. Add chicken; cook and stir 5 minutes or until chicken is golden. Add spinach and leek; cook and stir 1 to 2 minutes. Spoon mixture into unbaked pie crust; sprinkle with cheese and flour.

3. Whisk half-and-half, eggs, brandy, salt, pepper and nutmeg in medium bowl until well blended; pour over cheese.

4. Bake 35 to 40 minutes or until knife inserted into center comes out clean. Let stand 5 minutes before serving. Serve hot, cold or at room temperature.

Hawaiian-Style Burgers

Makes 6 servings

1½ **pounds ground beef**	⅓ **cup pineapple preserves**
⅓ **cup chopped green onions**	⅓ **cup barbecue sauce**
2 **tablespoons Worcestershire sauce**	6 **canned pineapple rings**
⅛ **teaspoon black pepper**	6 **hamburger buns, split and toasted**

1. Combine beef, green onions, Worcestershire sauce and pepper in large bowl. Shape into six ½-inch-thick patties.

2. Combine preserves and barbecue sauce in small saucepan. Bring to a boil over medium heat, stirring frequently.

3. Spray grid with nonstick cooking spray. Prepare grill for direct cooking over medium heat. Grill patties, covered, 8 to 10 minutes (or uncovered, 13 to 15 minutes) to medium (160°F), turning and brushing often with sauce. Place pineapple on grid; grill 1 minute or until browned, turning once.

4. Serve patties and pineapple on buns.

Stuffed Hash Browns

Makes 1 to 2 servings

1½ **cups shredded potatoes***	½ **cup diced ham (¼-inch pieces)**
2 **tablespoons finely chopped onion**	3 **eggs**
¼ **teaspoon plus ⅛ teaspoon salt, divided**	2 **tablespoons milk**
⅛ **teaspoon black pepper**	2 **slices American cheese**
2 **tablespoons butter, divided**	*Use refrigerated shredded hash brown potatoes or shredded peeled russet potatoes, squeezed and blotted dry with paper towels.
1 **tablespoon vegetable oil**	

1. Preheat oven to 250°F. Place wire rack over baking sheet. Combine potatoes, onion, ¼ teaspoon salt and pepper in medium bowl; mix well.

2. Heat 1 tablespoon butter and oil in small (6- to 8-inch) nonstick skillet over medium heat. Add potato mixture; spread to cover bottom of skillet evenly, pressing down gently with spatula to flatten. Cook 10 minutes or until bottom and edges are golden brown. Cover skillet with large inverted plate; carefully flip hash browns onto plate. Slide hash browns back into skillet, cooked side up. Cook 10 minutes or until golden brown. Slide hash browns onto prepared wire rack; place in oven to keep warm while preparing ham and eggs.

3. Melt 1 teaspoon butter in same skillet over medium-high heat. Add ham; cook and stir 2 to 3 minutes or until lightly browned. Remove to plate.

4. Whisk eggs, milk and remaining ⅛ teaspoon salt in small bowl. Melt remaining 2 teaspoons butter in same skillet over medium-high heat. Add egg mixture; cook 3 minutes or just until eggs are cooked through, stirring to form large, fluffy curds. Place cheese slices on top of eggs; remove from heat and cover skillet with lid or foil to melt cheese.

5. Place hash brown on serving plate; sprinkle one side of hash brown with ham. Top ham with eggs; fold hash brown in half.

Egg Salad Sandwiches

Makes 4 servings

6 eggs

3 tablespoons mayonnaise

$\frac{1}{2}$ cup finely chopped celery

2 tablespoons chopped dill pickle or sweet pickle relish

$\frac{1}{8}$ to $\frac{1}{4}$ teaspoon salt

Black pepper (optional)

8 slices whole wheat bread

1. Bring medium saucepan of water to a boil. Gently add eggs with slotted spoon. Reduce heat to maintain a simmer; cook 12 minutes. Meanwhile, fill medium bowl with cold water and ice cubes. Drain eggs and place in ice water; cool 10 minutes.

2. Peel and chop eggs; place in medium bowl (or place in medium bowl and mash with fork). Stir in mayonnaise, celery, pickle and salt. Season to taste with black pepper.

3. Spread $\frac{1}{2}$ cup egg salad on each of four bread slices; top with remaining bread slices.

Dynamite Dinners

Spicy Buttermilk Oven-Fried Chicken

Makes 6 servings

1 whole chicken, cut up
   (about 4 pounds)

2 cups buttermilk

1½ cups all-purpose flour

1 teaspoon salt

1 teaspoon ground red
   pepper

½ teaspoon garlic powder

¼ cup canola or vegetable oil

1. Arrange chicken in single layer in 13×9-inch baking dish. Pour buttermilk over chicken. Cover with plastic wrap; marinate in refrigerator at least 2 hours.

2. Preheat oven to 350°F. Combine flour, salt, red pepper and garlic powder in large shallow bowl. Heat oil in large skillet over medium-high heat.

3. Drain chicken, discarding marinade. Coat chicken pieces with flour mixture. Place chicken in hot oil; cook about 10 minutes or until brown and crisp on all sides, turning once. Place chicken in single layer in clean 13×9-inch baking dish.

4. Bake 30 to 45 minutes or until chicken is cooked through (165°F).

Spaghetti & Meatballs

Makes 4 servings

Meatballs

- 1½ **pounds meatloaf mix***
- ½ **cup plain dry bread crumbs**
- ⅓ **cup grated onion**
- ⅓ **cup milk**
- ¼ **cup grated Parmesan cheese, plus additional for serving**
- 1 **egg**
- 2 **cloves garlic, minced**
- 1½ **teaspoons dried basil**
- 1 **teaspoon salt**
- 1 **teaspoon dried oregano**
- ½ **teaspoon dried sage**

Sauce

- 1½ **tablespoons olive oil**
- 3 **cloves garlic, minced**
- ¼ **cup tomato paste**
- 2 **teaspoons dried basil**
- ½ **teaspoon sugar**
- ¼ **teaspoon salt**
- 1 **can (28 ounces) whole tomatoes, undrained**
- 1 **package (16 ounces) uncooked spaghetti, cooked according to package directions**

*Meatloaf mix is a combination of ground beef, pork and veal. You can substitute 1 pound ground beef, ¼ pound ground pork and ¼ pound ground veal, ¾ pound each ground beef and pork or all ground beef.

1. Preheat oven to 400°F. Spray large baking pan with nonstick cooking spray. For meatballs, combine meat loaf mix, bread crumbs, onion, milk, ¼ cup cheese, egg, 2 cloves garlic, 1½ teaspoons dried basil, 1 teaspoon salt, oregano and sage in large bowl; mix lightly but thoroughly. Shape mixture by ⅓ cupfuls into balls.

2. Place meatballs on prepared pan; bake 25 to 30 minutes or until thermometer inserted into centers registers 145°F.

3. For sauce, heat oil in large saucepan over medium heat. Add 3 cloves garlic; cook and stir 1 minute. Stir in tomato paste, 2 teaspoons dried basil, sugar and ¼ teaspoon salt; cook and stir 1 minute. Add tomatoes; bring to a boil. Reduce heat to low; simmer, uncovered, 10 minutes, breaking up tomatoes with wooden spoon.

4. Add meatballs; cook over medium heat 8 to 10 minutes or until sauce is heated through and meatballs are cooked through (160°F), stirring occasionally. Serve meatballs and sauce over spaghetti with additional cheese.

Salisbury Steaks with Mushroom-Wine Sauce

Makes 4 servings

1½ **pounds ground beef**

½ **cup seasoned bread crumbs**

1 **egg**

2 **teaspoons Worcestershire sauce, divided**

1 **teaspoon dried mustard**

⅛ **teaspoon black pepper**

2 **tablespoons butter**

1 **package (8 ounces) sliced mushrooms**

2 **tablespoons sherry or vermouth**

1 **jar (12 ounces) *or* 1 can (10½ ounces) beef gravy**

1. Combine beef, bread crumbs, egg, 1 teaspoon Worcestershire sauce, mustard and pepper in medium bowl; mix well. Shape mixture into four (¼-inch-thick) oval patties.

2. Heat large nonstick skillet over medium-high heat. Place patties in skillet; cook 3 minutes per side or until browned. Transfer to plate. Pour off drippings.

3. Melt butter in same skillet over medium-high heat. Add mushrooms; cook and stir 2 minutes. Add sherry and remaining 1 teaspoon Worcestershire sauce; cook 1 minute. Add gravy; mix well.

4. Return patties to skillet; reduce heat to medium. Simmer, uncovered, 2 minutes or until cooked through (160°F), stirring occasionally.

Country Chicken Pot Pie

Makes 6 servings

Single-Crust Pie Pastry (page 187) *or* **1 refrigerated pie crust (half of 14-ounce package)**

2 **tablespoons butter**

1 **pound boneless skinless chicken breasts, cut into 1-inch pieces**

¾ **teaspoon salt**

8 **ounces fresh green beans, cut into 1-inch pieces (about 2 cups)**

½ **cup chopped red bell pepper**

½ **cup thinly sliced celery**

3 **tablespoons all-purpose flour**

½ **cup chicken broth**

½ **cup half-and-half**

1 **teaspoon dried thyme**

½ **teaspoon dried sage**

1 **cup frozen pearl onions**

½ **cup frozen corn**

1. Prepare pie pastry; roll into 12-inch circle. Refrigerate until ready to use.

2. Preheat oven to 425°F. Spray 10-inch deep-dish pie plate with nonstick cooking spray.

3. Melt butter in large skillet over medium-high heat. Add chicken; cook and stir 3 minutes or until no longer pink in center. Sprinkle with salt. Add green beans, bell pepper and celery; cook and stir 3 minutes or until vegetables are crisp-tender. Sprinkle evenly with flour; cook and stir 1 minute.

4. Stir in broth, half-and-half, thyme and sage; bring to a boil over high heat. Reduce heat to low; simmer 3 minutes or until sauce is thickened. Stir in onions and corn. Return to a simmer; cook and stir 1 minute.

5. Transfer mixture to prepared pie plate. Place prepared pie pastry over chicken mixture; turn edge under and crimp to seal. Cut slits in pie pastry to vent steam.

6. Bake 25 minutes or until crust is light golden brown and mixture is hot and bubbly. Let stand 5 minutes before serving.

Sloppy Joes

Makes 8 to 12 servings

3 **pounds ground beef**

1 **cup chopped onion**

1 **cup chopped red bell pepper**

3 **cloves garlic, minced**

1¼ **cups ketchup**

¼ **cup plus 1 tablespoon Worcestershire sauce**

¼ **cup packed brown sugar**

3 **tablespoons mustard**

3 **tablespoons cider vinegar**

2 **teaspoons chili powder**

Toasted hamburger buns

1. Cook beef, onion, bell pepper and garlic in large saucepan over medium-high heat 10 minutes or until meat is no longer pink, stirring to break up meat.

2. Add ketchup, Worcestershire sauce, brown sugar, mustard, vinegar and chili powder; mix well. Bring to a simmer; cook 10 minutes or until heated through.

3. Serve mixture on hamburger buns.

Swedish Meatballs

Makes 4 to 6 servings

1½ cups fresh bread crumbs
1 cup whipping cream
2 tablespoons butter, divided
1 small onion, chopped
1 pound ground beef*
½ pound ground pork*
3 tablespoons chopped fresh parsley, divided
1½ teaspoons salt

¼ teaspoon ground allspice
¼ teaspoon black pepper
1 cup beef broth
1 cup sour cream
1 tablespoon all-purpose flour
Hot cooked egg noodles

*Or use 1½ pounds meatloaf mix.

1. Combine bread crumbs and cream in large bowl; mix well. Let stand 10 minutes.

2. Melt 1 tablespoon butter in large skillet over medium heat. Add onion; cook and stir 5 minutes or until onion is tender. Add to bread crumb mixture with beef, pork, 2 tablespoons parsley, salt, allspice and pepper; mix well. Cover; refrigerate 1 hour.

3. Pat meat mixture into 1-inch-thick square on cutting board. Cut into 36 squares. Shape each square into a ball. Melt remaining 1 tablespoon butter in large skillet over medium heat. Add meatballs; cook 10 minutes or until browned on all sides and no longer pink in centers (160°F). Remove meatballs to paper towel-lined plate to drain. Drain drippings from skillet.

4. Pour broth into same skillet. Heat over medium-high heat, stirring frequently and scraping up any browned bits from bottom of skillet. Reduce heat to low.

5. Combine sour cream and flour in small bowl; mix well. Stir sour cream mixture into skillet; cook 5 minutes, stirring constantly. *Do not boil.* Add meatballs; cook 5 minutes. Serve meatballs and sauce over noodles; sprinkle with remaining 1 tablespoon parsley.

Beef Wellington

6 center-cut beef tenderloin steaks, 1 inch thick (about 2½ pounds)

¾ teaspoon salt, divided

½ teaspoon black pepper, divided

2 tablespoons butter

8 ounces cremini or button mushrooms, finely chopped

¼ cup finely chopped shallots

2 tablespoons ruby port or sweet Madeira wine

1 package (about 17 ounces) frozen puff pastry, thawed

1 egg, separated

½ cup (4 ounces) prepared liver pâté*

2 teaspoons water

*Pâté can be found in the gourmet or deli section of most supermarkets or in specialty food stores.

1. Sprinkle steaks with ½ teaspoon salt and ¼ teaspoon pepper. Heat large skillet over medium-high heat. Cook steaks in batches about 3 minutes per side or until well browned and instant-read thermometer inserted into center of steaks registers 110°F (very rare). Remove to plate; set aside to cool.

2. Melt butter in same skillet over medium heat. Add mushrooms and shallots; cook and stir 5 minutes or until mushrooms are tender. Add port, remaining ¼ teaspoon salt and ¼ teaspoon pepper; bring to a boil. Reduce heat to low; simmer 10 minutes or until liquid evaporates, stirring frequently. Remove from heat; cool completely.

3. Roll out each pastry sheet on lightly floured surface to 18×10-inch rectangle with lightly floured rolling pin. Cut each sheet into three 10×6-inch rectangles. Cut small amount of pastry from corners to use for decoration, if desired.

4. Whisk egg white in small bowl until foamy; brush over each pastry rectangle. Place one cooled steak on each pastry rectangle. Spread pâté evenly over steaks. Top with mushroom mixture; press lightly to adhere.

5. Fold pastry over steak; press edges to seal. Cut pastry scraps into shapes and use to decorate; if desired. Place steaks on ungreased baking sheet.

6. Whisk egg yolk and water in small bowl. Brush pastry with egg yolk mixture. Cover loosely with plastic wrap; refrigerate 1 to 4 hours before baking.

7. Preheat oven to 400°F. Bake 20 to 25 minutes or until pastry is puffed and golden brown and steaks are medium (145°F). Let stand 10 minutes before serving.

Sweet & Saucy Ribs

Makes 4 servings

2 pounds pork baby back ribs	1 jar (8 ounces) cherry jam or preserves
1 teaspoon black pepper	1 tablespoon Dijon mustard
2½ cups barbecue sauce (not mesquite flavored)	¼ teaspoon salt

Slow Cooker Directions

1. Trim excess fat from ribs. Rub 1 teaspoon pepper over ribs. Cut ribs into 2-rib portions; place in slow cooker.

2. Combine barbecue sauce, jam, mustard and ¼ teaspoon salt in small bowl; pour over ribs.

3. Cover; cook on LOW 6 to 8 hours or until ribs are tender. Season with additional salt and pepper, if desired. Serve ribs with sauce.

Weeknight Chicken Tacos

Makes 6 to 8 servings

2 pounds boneless skinless chicken thighs

Salt and black pepper

1 tablespoon vegetable oil

1 cup chicken broth or water

1 cup chunky salsa

Corn tortillas, warmed

1 cup shredded lettuce

1 cup pico de gallo

1 cup (4 ounces) shredded taco blend or Cheddar cheese

Optional toppings: sour cream, sliced jalapeño peppers and/or diced avocado

1. Season chicken with salt and black pepper. Heat oil in large saucepan over medium-high heat. Add chicken; cook about 5 minutes per side or until lightly browned. Add broth and salsa; cook 1 minute, scraping up browned bits from bottom of saucepan. Bring to a boil. Reduce heat to medium-low; cover and cook about 35 minutes or until chicken is cooked through (165°F).

2. Remove chicken to plate; let stand 5 to 10 minutes or until cool enough to handle. Meanwhile, cook liquid remaining in saucepan over medium heat 5 to 10 minutes or until slightly thickened.

3. Shred chicken into bite-size pieces with two forks. Return to saucepan; stir to coat with sauce. Serve chicken mixture in tortillas with lettuce, pico de gallo, cheese and desired toppings.

Milanese Pork Chops

Makes 4 servings

2 tablespoons all-purpose flour	¼ cup grated Parmesan cheese
½ teaspoon salt	4 boneless pork loin chops, ¾ inch thick
½ teaspoon black pepper	
1 egg	1 tablespoon olive oil
1 teaspoon water	1 tablespoon butter
¼ cup seasoned dry bread crumbs	Lemon wedges

1. Preheat oven to 400°F. Combine flour, salt and pepper in shallow bowl. Beat egg and water in second shallow bowl. Combine bread crumbs and Parmesan cheese in third shallow bowl.

2. Coat both sides of pork with flour mixture. Dip both sides of pork in egg mixture, letting excess drip back into bowl. Roll in bread crumb mixture to coat, pressing coating onto pork. Place on waxed paper-lined plate; refrigerate 15 minutes.

3. Heat oil and butter in large ovenproof skillet over medium-high heat until bubbly. Add pork; cook 4 minutes or until golden brown. Turn pork and transfer skillet to oven. Bake 6 to 8 minutes or until cooked through (145°F). Serve with lemon wedges.

Pasta with Creamy Vodka Sauce

Makes 4 servings

12 ounces uncooked campanelle or penne pasta	1 cup whipping cream
2 tablespoons butter	½ teaspoon salt
6 plum tomatoes, seeded and chopped	¼ teaspoon red pepper flakes
4 cloves garlic, minced	⅔ cup grated Parmesan cheese
6 tablespoons vodka	2 tablespoons snipped fresh chives

1. Cook pasta in large saucepan of salted boiling water according to package directions for al dente. Drain and return to saucepan; keep warm.

2. Meanwhile, melt butter in large skillet over medium heat. Add tomatoes and garlic; cook 3 minutes, stirring frequently. Add vodka; simmer 2 minutes or until most of liquid has evaporated.

3. Stir in cream, salt and red pepper flakes; simmer 2 to 3 minutes or until slightly thickened. Remove from heat; let stand 2 minutes. Stir in Parmesan cheese until melted.

4. Add sauce and chives to pasta; toss to coat. Serve immediately.

Meatloaf

Makes 6 to 8 servings

1 tablespoon vegetable oil	1 pound ground beef*
2 green onions, minced	1 pound ground pork*
1/4 cup minced green bell pepper	1 cup plain dry bread crumbs
1/4 cup grated carrot	2 teaspoons salt
3 cloves garlic, minced	1/2 teaspoon onion powder
3/4 cup milk	1/2 teaspoon black pepper
2 eggs	1/2 cup ketchup, divided
	*Or use 2 pounds meatloaf mix.

1. Preheat oven to 350°F.

2. Heat oil in large skillet over medium-high heat. Add green onions, bell pepper, carrot and garlic; cook and stir 5 minutes or until vegetables are softened.

3. Whisk milk and eggs in medium bowl until well blended. Gently mix beef, pork, bread crumbs, salt, onion powder and black pepper in large bowl with hands. Add milk mixture, vegetables and 1/4 cup ketchup; mix gently but thoroughly. Press into 9×5-inch loaf pan; place pan on rimmed baking sheet.

4. Bake 30 minutes. Spread remaining 1/4 cup ketchup over meatloaf; bake 1 hour or until cooked through (160°F). Cool in pan 10 minutes; cut into slices.

Crazy for Casseroles

Heartland Chicken Casserole

Makes 6 servings

10 slices white bread, cubed

1½ cups cracker crumbs or plain dry bread crumbs, divided

4 cups cubed cooked chicken

3 cups chicken broth

1 cup chopped onion

1 cup chopped celery

1 can (8 ounces) sliced mushrooms, drained

1 jar (about 4 ounces) pimientos, drained and diced

3 eggs, lightly beaten

Salt and black pepper

1 tablespoon butter

1. Preheat oven to 350°F. Grease 2½-quart baking dish.

2. Combine bread cubes and 1 cup cracker crumbs in large bowl. Add chicken, broth, onion, celery, mushrooms, pimientos and eggs; mix well. Season with salt and pepper; spoon into prepared baking dish.

3. Melt butter in small saucepan over low heat. Add remaining ½ cup cracker crumbs; cook and stir until golden. Sprinkle crumbs over casserole. Bake 1 hour or until hot and bubbly.

Seafood Newburg Casserole

Makes 6 servings

1 can (10½ ounces) condensed cream of shrimp soup, undiluted

½ cup half-and-half

1 tablespoon dry sherry

¼ teaspoon ground red pepper

2 cans (6 ounces each) lump crabmeat, drained

3 cups cooked rice

4 ounces medium raw shrimp, peeled

4 ounces bay scallops, rinsed and patted dry

1 jar (4 ounces) pimientos, drained and chopped

2 tablespoons finely chopped fresh parsley

1. Preheat oven to 350°F. Grease 2½-quart baking dish.

2. Whisk soup, half-and-half, sherry and red pepper in large bowl until blended. Pick out and discard any shell or cartilage from crabmeat. Add crabmeat, rice, shrimp, scallops and pimientos to soup mixture; mix well. Transfer mixture to prepared baking dish.

3. Cover and bake 25 minutes or until shrimp and scallops are opaque. Sprinkle with parsley.

Green Bean Casserole

Makes 6 to 8 servings

1 **pound fresh green beans, cut into 2-inch pieces**

2 **tablespoons vegetable oil**

1 **onion, finely chopped**

1 **package (8 ounces) cremini mushrooms, chopped**

1 **can (10$\frac{1}{2}$ ounces) condensed cream of mushroom soup, undiluted**

$\frac{1}{2}$ **cup milk**

$\frac{1}{4}$ **teaspoon black pepper**

$\frac{1}{2}$ **(6-ounce) package French fried onions (about 1$\frac{1}{3}$ cups), divided**

1. Preheat oven to 350°F. Grease 2$\frac{1}{2}$-quart baking dish.

2. Cook green beans in large saucepan of salted boiling water 4 minutes or until crisp-tender; drain.

3. Heat oil in large skillet over medium-high heat. Add chopped onions; cook and stir 5 to 7 minutes or until softened and lightly browned. Add mushrooms; cook and stir 8 minutes or until browned.

4. Combine soup, milk and pepper in large bowl; stir in beans and mushroom mixture. Fold in half of fried onions; spread in prepared baking dish.

5. Bake 30 minutes. Stir green bean mixture; sprinkle with remaining fried onions. Bake 5 to 7 minutes or until onions are golden brown.

Mac & Cheesiest

Makes about 6 servings

8 ounces uncooked elbow macaroni	1/4 teaspoon black pepper
1/4 cup (1/2 stick) butter	2 cups (8 ounces) shredded Cheddar cheese, divided
5 tablespoons all-purpose flour	1/2 cup (2 ounces) shredded Gruyère or Swiss cheese
2 3/4 cups warm milk	1/2 cup (2 ounces) shredded American cheese
1 teaspoon salt	3/4 cup (3 ounces) shredded aged Gouda cheese
1/4 teaspoon ground nutmeg	

1. Preheat oven to 350°F. Cook pasta in large saucepan of boiling salted water according to package directions until barely al dente. Run under cold water to stop cooking; drain.

2. Meanwhile, melt butter in another large saucepan or deep skillet over medium heat until bubbly. Whisk in flour until smooth paste forms; cook and stir 2 minutes without browning. Gradually whisk in milk; cook 6 to 8 minutes or until mixture begins to bubble and thickens slightly, whisking frequently. Add salt, nutmeg and black pepper.

3. Remove from heat. Add 1 1/2 cups Cheddar, Gruyère, American and Gouda cheeses by handfuls, stirring until melted after each addition. Stir pasta into cheese sauce. Pour into 2-quart baking dish; sprinkle with remaining 1/2 cup Cheddar cheese.

4. Bake 20 to 30 minutes or until cheese is golden brown and sauce is bubbly.

Barbecue Chicken with Corn Bread Topper

Makes 8 servings

1½ **pounds diced cooked chicken**

1 **can (about 15 ounces) kidney beans, rinsed and drained**

1 **cup chopped green bell pepper**

1 **can (8 ounces) tomato sauce**

½ **cup barbecue sauce**

1 **package (6 ounces) corn bread mix, plus ingredients to prepare mix**

1. Preheat oven to 375°F. Grease 8-inch baking dish.

2. Combine chicken, beans, bell pepper, tomato sauce and barbecue sauce in large skillet. Cook over medium heat 6 to 8 minutes or until heated through, stirring occasionally. Pour into prepared baking dish.

3. Meanwhile, prepare corn bread mix according to package directions. Spoon batter over chicken mixture.

4. Bake 15 to 18 minutes or until toothpick inserted into center of corn bread comes out clean.

Wild Rice & Chicken Casserole

Makes 4 to 6 servings

1 package (6 ounces) long
   grain and wild rice mix

2 tablespoons butter

1/2 cup chopped onion

1/2 cup chopped celery

2 cups cubed cooked chicken

1 can (10 1/2 ounces)
   condensed cream
   of mushroom soup,
   undiluted

1/2 cup sour cream

1/3 cup dry white wine

1/2 teaspoon curry powder

1. Preheat oven to 350°F.

2. Prepare rice mix according to package directions.

3. Meanwhile, melt butter in large skillet over medium heat. Add onion and celery; cook and stir 5 to 7 minutes until tender. Stir in rice mix, chicken, soup, sour cream, wine and curry powder. Spread mixture in 2-quart baking dish.

4. Bake 40 minutes or until heated through.

Hearty Hash Brown Casserole

Makes about 16 servings

2 cups sour cream

2 cups (8 ounces) shredded Colby cheese, divided

1 can (10½ ounces) cream of celery or chicken soup, undiluted

½ cup (1 stick) butter, melted

1 small onion, finely chopped

¾ teaspoon salt

½ teaspoon black pepper

1 package (30 ounces) frozen shredded hash brown potatoes, thawed

1. Preheat oven to 375°F. Grease 13×9-inch baking dish.

2. Combine sour cream, 1½ cups cheese, soup, butter, onion, salt and pepper in large bowl; mix well. Add potatoes; stir until well blended. Spread mixture in prepared baking dish. (Do not pack down.) Sprinkle with remaining ½ cup cheese.

3. Bake 45 minutes or until cheese is melted and top of casserole is beginning to brown.

Classic Lasagna

Makes 6 to 8 servings

1 tablespoon olive oil

8 ounces bulk mild Italian sausage

8 ounces ground beef

1 medium onion, chopped

3 cloves garlic, minced, divided

1½ teaspoons salt, divided

1 can (28 ounces) crushed tomatoes

1 can (28 ounces) diced tomatoes

2 teaspoons Italian seasoning

1 egg

1 container (15 ounces) ricotta cheese

¾ cup grated Parmesan cheese, divided

½ cup minced fresh parsley

¼ teaspoon black pepper

12 uncooked no-boil lasagna noodles

4 cups (16 ounces) shredded mozzarella

1. Preheat oven to 350°F. Grease 13×9-inch baking dish.

2. Heat oil in large saucepan over medium-high heat. Add sausage, beef, onion, 2 cloves garlic and 1 teaspoon salt; cook and stir 10 minutes or until meat is no longer pink, breaking up meat with wooden spoon. Add crushed tomatoes, diced tomatoes and Italian seasoning; bring to a boil. Reduce heat to medium-low; cook 15 minutes, stirring occasionally.

3. Meanwhile, beat egg in medium bowl. Stir in ricotta, ½ cup Parmesan, parsley, remaining 1 clove garlic, ½ teaspoon salt and pepper until well blended.

4. Spread ¼ cup sauce in prepared baking dish. Top with 3 noodles. Spread one third of ricotta mixture over noodles. Sprinkle with 1 cup mozzarella; top with 2 cups sauce. Repeat layers of noodles, ricotta mixture, mozzarella and sauce two times. Top with remaining 3 noodles, sauce, 1 cup mozzarella and ¼ cup Parmesan. Cover dish with foil sprayed with cooking spray.

5. Bake 30 minutes. Remove foil; bake 10 to 15 minutes or until hot and bubbly. Let stand 10 minutes before serving.

Tuna-Macaroni Casserole

Makes 6 servings

1 cup mayonnaise

1 cup (4 ounces) shredded Swiss cheese

½ cup milk

¼ cup chopped onion

¼ cup chopped red bell pepper

⅛ teaspoon black pepper

2 cans (about 6 ounces each) tuna, drained and flaked

1 package (about 10 ounces) frozen peas

2 cups shell medium pasta or elbow macaroni, cooked and drained

½ cup dry bread crumbs

2 tablespoons melted butter

Chopped fresh parsley (optional)

1. Preheat oven to 350°F. Grease 2-quart baking dish.

2. Combine mayonnaise, cheese, milk, onion, bell pepper and black pepper in large bowl. Add tuna, peas and pasta; mix well. Spread in prepared baking dish.

3. Mix bread crumbs with butter in small bowl; sprinkle over top of casserole. Bake 30 to 40 minutes or until heated through. Top with chopped parsley.

Old-Fashioned Herb Stuffing

Makes 4 servings

6 slices (8 ounces) whole wheat, rye or white bread (or a combination), cut into 1/2-inch cubes

1 tablespoon butter

1 cup chopped onion

1/2 cup thinly sliced celery

1/2 cup thinly sliced carrot

1 cup vegetable or chicken broth

1 tablespoon chopped fresh thyme *or* 1 teaspoon dried thyme

1 tablespoon chopped fresh sage *or* 1 teaspoon dried sage

1/2 teaspoon salt

1/2 teaspoon paprika

1/4 teaspoon black pepper

1. Preheat oven to 350°F. Grease 1½-quart baking dish.

2. Place bread cubes on baking sheet; bake 10 minutes or until dry.

3. Melt butter in large saucepan over medium heat. Add onion, celery and carrot; cook and stir 10 minutes or until vegetables are tender. Add broth, thyme, sage, salt, paprika and pepper; bring to a simmer. Stir in bread cubes. Spoon into prepared baking dish.

4. Cover and bake 25 to 30 minutes or until heated through.

It's a Keeper Casserole

Makes 4 servings

1 tablespoon vegetable oil

½ cup chopped onion

¼ cup chopped green bell pepper

1 clove garlic, minced

2 tablespoons all-purpose flour

1 teaspoon sugar

½ teaspoon salt

½ teaspoon dried basil

½ teaspoon black pepper

1 package (about 16 ounces) frozen meatballs, thawed

1 can (about 14 ounces) whole tomatoes, cut up and drained

1½ cups cooked vegetables (green beans, corn, peas, broccoli and/or carrots)

1 teaspoon beef bouillon granules

1 teaspoon Worcestershire sauce

1 can (12 ounces) refrigerated buttermilk biscuits

1. Preheat oven to 400°F. Heat oil in large saucepan over medium heat. Add onion, bell pepper and garlic; cook and stir 5 minutes or until vegetables are tender.

2. Stir in flour, sugar, salt, basil and black pepper; mix well. Add meatballs, tomatoes, vegetables, bouillon and Worcestershire sauce; cook and stir until slightly thickened and bubbly. Pour into 2-quart baking dish.

3. Place biscuits on top of casserole. Bake 15 minutes or until biscuits are golden brown.

 Tip Use whatever meat you have on hand instead of the meatballs—ground beef or turkey, cut-up sausage or hot dogs or chopped cooked chicken.

Reuben Noodle Bake

Makes 6 servings

8 ounces uncooked egg noodles

5 ounces thinly sliced deli-style corned beef

2 cups (8 ounces) shredded Swiss cheese

1 can (about 14 ounces) sauerkraut with caraway seeds, drained

$\frac{1}{2}$ cup Thousand Island dressing

$\frac{1}{2}$ cup milk

1 tablespoon prepared mustard

2 slices pumpernickel bread

1 tablespoon butter, melted

1. Preheat oven to 350°F. Grease 13×9-inch baking dish. Cook noodles in large saucepan of salted boiling water according to package directions for al dente; drain.

2. Meanwhile, cut corned beef into bite-size pieces. Combine noodles, corned beef, cheese and sauerkraut in large bowl. Spread in prepared baking dish.

3. Combine dressing, milk and mustard in small bowl. Spoon evenly over noodle mixture.

4. Tear bread into large pieces; process in food processor or blender until crumbs form. Add butter; pulse to combine. Sprinkle over casserole.

5. Bake 25 to 30 minutes or until heated through.

Beef Stroganoff Casserole

Makes 6 servings

1 **pound ground beef**	1/4 **cup dry white wine**
1/4 **teaspoon salt**	1 **can (10 1/2 ounces) condensed cream of mushroom soup, undiluted**
1/8 **teaspoon black pepper**	
1 **teaspoon vegetable oil**	
1 **package (8 ounces) sliced mushrooms**	1/2 **cup sour cream**
	1 **tablespoon Dijon mustard**
1 **large onion, chopped**	4 **cups cooked egg noodles**
3 **cloves garlic, minced**	**Chopped fresh parsley**

1. Preheat oven to 350°F. Grease 13×9-inch baking dish.

2. Heat large skillet over medium-high heat. Add beef; season with salt and pepper. Cook 6 to 8 minutes or until browned, stirring to break up meat. Drain fat; place beef in large bowl.

3. Heat oil in same skillet over medium-high heat. Add mushrooms, onion and garlic; cook and stir 2 minutes or until onion is tender. Add wine. Reduce heat to medium-low; simmer 3 minutes. Remove from heat; stir in soup, sour cream and mustard until well blended. Return beef to skillet; stir to blend.

4. Place noodles in prepared baking dish. Pour beef mixture over noodles; stir until noodles are well coated.

5. Bake 30 minutes or until heated through. Sprinkle with parsley just before serving.

Spinach-Cheese Pasta Casserole

Makes 6 to 8 servings

12 ounces uncooked medium
  shell pasta

2 eggs

1 cup ricotta cheese

1 package (10 ounces) frozen
  chopped spinach, thawed
  and squeezed dry

1 teaspoon salt

1 jar (26 ounces) marinara
  sauce

1 cup (4 ounces) shredded
  mozzarella cheese

¼ cup grated Parmesan
  cheese

1. Preheat oven to 350°F. Grease 1½-quart baking dish.

2. Cook pasta in large saucepan of salted boiling water according to package directions for al dente.

3. Whisk eggs in large bowl until blended. Add ricotta, spinach and salt; stir until blended. Stir in pasta and marinara sauce; mix well. Spread in prepared baking dish; sprinkle with mozzarella and Parmesan.

4. Cover and bake 30 minutes. Uncover and bake 15 minutes or until hot and bubbly.

Pastitsio

Makes 6 servings

1 pound ground beef or lamb	3 tablespoons butter
1½ cups mild picante sauce	3 tablespoons all-purpose flour
1 can (8 ounces) tomato sauce	1½ cups milk
1 tablespoon sugar	½ teaspoon salt
½ teaspoon ground allspice	¼ teaspoon black pepper
½ teaspoon ground cinnamon	2 eggs
¼ teaspoon ground nutmeg, divided	½ cup grated Parmesan cheese
8 ounces uncooked elbow macaroni	

1. Preheat oven to 350°F. Grease 9-inch square baking dish.

2. Brown beef in large skillet over medium-high heat 6 to 8 minutes, stirring to break up meat. Drain fat. Add picante sauce, tomato sauce, sugar, allspice, cinnamon and ⅛ teaspoon nutmeg; bring to a boil. Reduce heat to low; cook 10 minutes, stirring frequently.

3. Meanwhile, cook pasta in large saucepan of salted boiling water according to package directions for al dente; drain. Place in prepared baking dish.

4. Melt butter in medium saucepan over medium heat. Add flour; whisk until smooth. Add milk, salt and pepper; cook and stir until thickened. Remove from heat. Whisk eggs in small bowl; whisk in ½ cup white sauce until blended. Add egg mixture to remaining white sauce in saucepan. Stir in Parmesan.

5. Stir ½ cup sauce into macaroni. Spread meat mixture over macaroni; top with remaining sauce. Sprinkle with remaining ⅛ teaspoon nutmeg.

6. Bake 30 to 40 minutes or until knife inserted into center comes out clean. Let stand 15 to 20 minutes before serving.

Hungarian Goulash Casserole

Makes 4 to 6 servings

1 package (12 ounces) egg noodles	1 cup sour cream, divided
1 pound ground pork	1 tablespoon cornstarch
1/4 teaspoon salt	1 can (10 1/2 ounces) cream of celery soup, undiluted
1/4 teaspoon ground nutmeg	1 cup milk
1/4 teaspoon black pepper	1 teaspoon sweet Hungarian paprika
1 tablespoon vegetable oil	2 teaspoons minced fresh dill

1. Preheat oven to 325°F. Grease 3-quart baking dish. Cook noodles in large saucepan of salted boiling water according to package directions for al dente. Drain and spread in prepared baking dish.

2. Combine pork, salt, nutmeg and pepper in medium bowl; shape into 1-inch balls. Heat oil in large skillet over medium-high heat. Add meatballs; cook 10 minutes or until browned on all sides and no longer pink in center. Place meatballs on noodles. Drain and discard drippings from skillet.

3. Stir 1/4 cup sour cream and cornstarch in small bowl until well blended; add to skillet. Stir in remaining 3/4 cup sour cream, soup, milk and paprika. Cook and stir over medium heat until smooth. *Do not boil.* Pour sauce over meatballs and noodles.

4. Bake 20 minutes or until heated through. Garnish with dill.

Chocolate Cereal Bars

Makes 2 dozen bars

6 cups crisp rice cereal	2 tablespoons butter
1 jar (7 ounces) marshmallow creme	1 teaspoon vanilla
1 cup semisweet chocolate chips	

1. Grease 13×9-inch baking pan. Place cereal in large heatproof bowl.

2. Melt marshmallow creme, chocolate chips and butter in medium heavy saucepan over medium heat, stirring occasionally. Remove from heat; stir in vanilla.

3. Pour chocolate mixture over cereal; stir until blended. Press into prepared pan. Cool completely; cut into squares.

Grandma's Old-Fashioned Oatmeal Cookies

Makes 4 to 5 dozen cookies

3½ cups all-purpose flour	2 cups sugar
3 cups old-fashioned oats	1 cup shortening
1 teaspoon baking soda	2 eggs
1 teaspoon salt	1 cup buttermilk
1 teaspoon ground cinnamon	1 cup raisins

1. Preheat oven to 350°F. Lightly grease cookie sheets or line with parchment paper. Whisk flour, oats, baking soda, salt and cinnamon in medium bowl.

2. Beat sugar and shortening in large bowl with electric mixer at medium speed until creamy. Beat in eggs, one at a time, until mixture is light and fluffy. With mixer running at low speed, add flour mixture in three additions alternately with buttermilk until well blended. Stir in raisins. Drop dough by rounded tablespoonfuls onto prepared cookie sheets.

3. Bake 12 minutes or until lightly browned. Cool on cookie sheets 2 minutes. Remove to wire racks; cool completely.

Black Forest Cake

Makes 12 servings

1 package (about 15 ounces) chocolate cake mix, plus ingredients to prepare mix

2 cans (20 ounces each) tart pitted cherries, undrained

1 cup sugar

1/4 cup cornstarch

1 1/2 teaspoons vanilla

3 cups cold whipping cream

1/3 cup powdered sugar

1. Preheat oven to 350°F. Grease and flour two 9-inch round cake pans. Prepare cake mix according to package directions. Divide batter between prepared pans.

2. Bake 30 to 35 minutes or until toothpick inserted into centers comes out clean. Cool in pans on wire racks 10 minutes. Remove to racks; cool completely.

3. Meanwhile, drain cherries, reserving 1/2 cup juice. Combine reserved juice, cherries, sugar and cornstarch in medium saucepan. Cook over low heat until thickened, stirring constantly. Stir in vanilla.

4. For frosting, combine whipping cream and powdered sugar in large bowl of stand mixer; attach whisk attachment. Whip at high speed 1 to 2 minutes or until stiff peaks form. Set aside 1 1/2 cups whipped cream for decorating cake.

5. Split each cake layer in half horizontally with long serrated knife. Crumble one layer; set aside. Place one cake layer on cake plate. Spread with 1 cup whipped cream; top with 3/4 cup cherry topping. Top with second cake layer; repeat layers of whipped cream and cherry topping. Top with third cake layer.

6. Frost top and side of cake with remaining whipped cream. Pat reserved crumbs onto side of cake. Spoon reserved whipped cream into piping bag fitted with star tip. Pipe whipped cream around edge of cake. Spoon remaining cherry topping onto top of cake.

Brown Sugar Fudge (Penuche)

Makes about 1 pound fudge

1⅓ cups granulated sugar	¼ cup (½ stick) butter, thinly sliced
1⅓ cups whipping cream	½ cup white chocolate chips
⅔ cup packed brown sugar	½ cup chopped walnuts
1 tablespoon light corn syrup	

1. Butter 8-inch square pan.

2. Combine granulated sugar, whipping cream, brown sugar and corn syrup in large heavy saucepan. Cook over medium heat, stirring constantly, until sugar dissolves and mixture comes to a boil. Attach candy thermometer to side of saucepan. Continue to cook until mixture reaches soft-ball stage (238°F), stirring occasionally.

3. Remove from heat. Add butter to saucepan; let stand about 10 minutes without stirring. Add white chocolate chips and nuts; stir until chips are completely melted. Spread in prepared pan. Refrigerate until firm. Cut into squares. Store in refrigerator.

Creamy Lemon Cheesecake

Makes 12 servings

9 graham crackers, crushed into crumbs

$1/3$ cup ground blanched almonds

6 tablespoons butter, melted

$3/4$ cup plus 2 tablespoons sugar, divided

3 packages (8 ounces each) cream cheese, softened

1 container (15 ounces) ricotta cheese

4 eggs

2 tablespoons finely grated lemon peel

1 teaspoon lemon extract

1 teaspoon vanilla

1. Preheat oven to 375°F.

2. Combine graham cracker crumbs, almonds, butter and 2 tablespoons sugar in medium bowl; mix well. Press evenly onto bottom and $1/2$ inch up side of 9-inch springform pan. Bake 5 minutes. Remove to wire rack to cool. *Reduce oven temperature to 325°F.*

3. Beat cream cheese, ricotta, eggs, remaining $3/4$ cup sugar, lemon peel, lemon extract and vanilla in large bowl with electric mixer at low speed until blended. Beat at high speed 4 to 5 minutes until smooth and creamy. Pour into crust.

4. Bake 1 hour and 10 minutes or until center is just set. *Do not overbake.* Remove to wire rack; cool to room temperature. Cover; refrigerate at least 4 hours or overnight.

Carrot Cake

Makes 12 to 16 servings

Cake

- 2 cups all-purpose flour
- 2 teaspoons baking soda
- 2 teaspoons ground cinnamon
- 1 teaspoon salt
- 4 eggs
- 2¼ cups granulated sugar
- 1 cup vegetable oil
- 1 cup buttermilk
- 1 tablespoon vanilla
- 3 medium carrots, shredded (3 cups)
- 3 cups walnuts, chopped and toasted,* divided
- 1 cup shredded coconut
- 1 can (8 ounces) crushed pineapple

Frosting

- 2 packages (8 ounces each) cream cheese, softened
- 1 cup (2 sticks) butter, softened
- Pinch of salt
- 3 cups powdered sugar
- 1 tablespoon orange juice
- 2 teaspoons grated orange peel
- 1 teaspoon vanilla

*To toast walnuts, spread on ungreased baking sheet. Bake in preheated 350°F oven 6 to 8 minutes or until lightly browned, stirring frequently.

1. Preheat oven to 350°F. Grease and flour two 9-inch round cake pans; line bottoms with parchment paper.

2. For cake, whisk flour, baking soda, cinnamon and 1 teaspoon salt in medium bowl. Whisk eggs in large bowl until blended. Add granulated sugar, oil, buttermilk and 1 tablespoon vanilla; whisk until well blended. Add flour mixture; stir until well blended. Add carrots, 1 cup walnuts, coconut and pineapple; stir just until blended. Divide batter evenly between prepared pans.

3. Bake 25 to 30 minutes or until toothpick inserted into centers comes out clean. Cool in pans 10 minutes. Remove to wire racks; cool completely.

4. For frosting, beat cream cheese, butter and pinch of salt in large bowl with electric mixer at medium speed 3 minutes or until creamy. Add powdered sugar, orange juice, orange peel and 1 teaspoon vanilla; beat at low speed until blended. Beat at medium speed 2 minutes or until frosting is smooth.

5. Place one cake layer on serving plate; spread with 2 cups frosting. Top with second layer; frost top and side of cake with remaining frosting. Press 1¾ cups walnuts onto side of cake. Sprinkle remaining ¼ cup walnuts over top of cake.

Snickerdoodles

Makes about 3 dozen cookies

¾ cup plus 2 tablespoons sugar, divided

2 teaspoons ground cinnamon, divided

1⅓ cups all-purpose flour

1 teaspoon cream of tartar

½ teaspoon baking soda

½ teaspoon salt

½ cup (1 stick) butter, softened

1 egg

1. Preheat oven to 375°F. Line cookie sheets with parchment paper. Combine 2 tablespoons sugar and 1 teaspoon cinnamon in small bowl.

2. Whisk flour, remaining 1 teaspoon cinnamon, cream of tartar, baking soda and salt in medium bowl.

3. Beat remaining ¾ cup sugar and butter in large bowl with electric mixer at medium speed about 3 minutes or until creamy. Beat in egg until well blended. Gradually add flour mixture, beating at low speed until stiff dough forms. Roll dough into 1-inch balls; roll in cinnamon-sugar mixture to coat. Place on prepared cookie sheets.

4. Bake 10 minutes or until cookies are set. *Do not overbake.* Remove to wire racks; cool completely.

Chocolate Rum Cake

Makes 10 to 12 servings

Cake

- 1 cup chopped pecans
- 1 package (12 ounces) semisweet chocolate chips
- 1 package (8 ounces) cream cheese, softened
- 1 package (about 15 ounces) yellow cake mix
- 1 package (4-serving size) vanilla instant pudding and pie filling mix
- 5 eggs
- ½ cup vegetable oil
- ½ cup cold water
- 3 tablespoons dark rum
- 1 teaspoon vanilla

Rum Butter Glaze

- ½ cup (1 stick) butter
- 1 cup sugar
- ¼ cup water
- 3 tablespoons dark rum
- 1 teaspoon vanilla
- Ice cream (optional)

1. Preheat oven to 325°F. Grease and flour 12-cup bundt or tube pan. Sprinkle pecans in bottom of pan.

2. Combine chocolate chips and cream cheese in medium microwavable bowl; microwave on MEDIUM (50%) 1 minute. Stir; microwave at additional 15-second intervals until mixture is melted and smooth. Set aside to cool.

3. Combine cake mix, pudding mix, eggs, oil, ½ cup water, 3 tablespoons rum and 1 teaspoon vanilla in large bowl; mix until smooth. Add cream cheese mixture; blend well. Pour batter into prepared pan.

4. Bake 45 to 50 minutes or until toothpick inserted near center comes out clean. *Do not overbake.* Cool in pan on wire rack 15 minutes.

5. For glaze, melt butter in medium saucepan over low heat. Add sugar and ¼ cup water; bring to a boil. Boil 5 minutes, stirring frequently. Remove from heat; let cool. Stir in 3 tablespoons rum and 1 teaspoon vanilla.

6. Spoon half of glaze over cake. Invert cake onto serving platter. Brush remaining glaze over top and side of cake using pastry brush. Wrap tightly in foil; let stand at least 1 hour. Serve with ice cream, if desired.

 For best flavor, leave this cake wrapped in foil for at least 24 hours before serving.

Pineapple Upside Down Cake

Makes 10 servings

Topping

- 1 small pineapple*
- ¼ cup (½ stick) butter
- ½ cup packed brown sugar
- Stemmed maraschino cherries

*Or substitute canned pineapple rings and proceed with step 2.

Cake

- 2 cups all-purpose flour
- 2 teaspoons baking powder
- ½ teaspoon baking soda
- ½ teaspoon salt
- ½ cup (1 stick) butter, softened
- 1 cup granulated sugar
- 1 egg
- 1 teaspoon vanilla
- 1 cup buttermilk

1. Preheat oven to 350°F. Spray 9-inch round baking pan with nonstick cooking spray. Remove top and bottom of pineapple. Cut off outside of pineapple and remove eyes. Cut pineapple crosswise into ¼-inch slices. Remove core with ½-inch cookie cutter or sharp knife.

2. For topping, cook and stir ¼ cup butter and brown sugar in medium skillet over medium heat until melted and smooth. Remove from heat. Pour into prepared pan. Arrange pineapple slices in pan, placing cherries in centers of pineapple. Reserve remaining pineapple for another use.

3. Whisk flour, baking powder, baking soda and salt in medium bowl. Beat ½ cup butter and granulated sugar in large bowl with electric mixer on medium speed until well blended. Beat in egg and vanilla. Add flour mixture alternately with buttermilk, mixing on low speed just until blended after each addition. Pour batter over pineapple.

4. Bake about 1 hour or until toothpick inserted into center comes out clean. Cool in pan on wire rack 10 minutes. Run thin knife around edge of pan to loosen cake. Invert onto serving plate; cool completely.

 Tip This cake can also be baked in a 12-inch cast iron skillet. Melt the butter and brown sugar in the skillet, add the pineapple and cherries and pour the batter over the fruit. Check the cake for doneness at 40 minutes.

Lemon Chiffon Cake

Makes about 12 servings

2 cups cake flour	1 teaspoon vanilla
1½ cups sugar	Grated peel of 1 lemon
1 tablespoon baking powder	½ teaspoon cream of tartar
¾ teaspoon salt	Lemon Glaze (recipe follows)
¾ cup cold water	Lemon slices (optional)
½ cup vegetable oil	
7 eggs, separated	

1. Preheat oven to 325°F. Whisk flour, sugar, baking powder and salt in medium bowl. Add water, oil, egg yolks, vanilla and lemon peel; stir until well blended.

2. Attach whisk attachment to electric mixer; whip egg whites and cream of tartar in large bowl at medium speed 2 to 3 minutes or until stiff peaks form. Gently fold in flour mixture just until blended. Pour batter into ungreased 10-inch tube pan.

3. Bake 60 to 70 minutes or until top springs back when lightly touched. Immediately invert cake onto clean glass bottle or funnel; cool completely in pan upside down.

4. Meanwhile, prepare glaze. Run knife or spatula around outer edge and inside tube to help release cake from pan. Invert cake onto serving plate. Drizzle with glaze; garnish with lemon slices.

Lemon Glaze: Whisk 1 cup powdered sugar and 1 tablespoon melted butter in small bowl. Whisk in 2 tablespoons lemon juice until well blended and smooth. Add additional lemon juice, 1 teaspoon at a time, if necessary to reach desired consistency.

Minty Shake

Makes 1 serving

2 cups French vanilla ice cream	10 drops green food coloring
½ cup milk, divided	Whipped cream and maraschino cherry (optional)
⅛ teaspoon peppermint extract	

Combine ice cream, ¼ cup milk, peppermint extract and green food coloring in blender; blend until smooth. Add additional ¼ cup milk if needed to reach desired consistency. Garnish with whipped cream and cherry.

Peanut Butter & Jelly Shakes

Makes 2 servings

1½ cups vanilla ice cream	6 peanut butter sandwich cookies, coarsely chopped
¼ cup milk	¼ cup strawberry preserves
2 tablespoons creamy peanut butter	1 to 2 teaspoons water

1. Combine ice cream, milk and peanut butter in blender. Process 1 minute or until smooth. Add chopped cookies; process 10 seconds. Pour into two glasses.

2. Place preserves and water in small bowl; stir until smooth. Stir 2 tablespoons preserve mixture into each glass. Serve immediately.

Strawberry Shortcake Layer Cake

Makes 12 to 16 servings

Cake

- 2 cups all-purpose flour
- 1½ cups granulated sugar
- 1 tablespoon baking powder
- 1 teaspoon baking soda
- ½ teaspoon salt
- 1 cup buttermilk
- ½ cup (1 stick) butter, cut into pieces, softened
- 3 eggs
- 1 teaspoon vanilla

Frosting

- 1 cup plus 1 tablespoon whipping cream, divided
- 1 cup powdered sugar
- 1 package (8 ounces) cream cheese, softened
- 1 cup granulated sugar
- ¼ cup (½ stick) butter, softened
- 1 teaspoon vanilla
- 2 containers (16 ounces each) fresh strawberries, stemmed and sliced

1. Preheat oven to 350°F. Grease and flour two 9-inch round cake pans; line bottoms with parchment paper.

2. Combine flour, 1½ cups granulated sugar, baking powder, baking soda and salt in bowl of electric mixer; mix at low speed 1 minute. Add buttermilk and butter; mix on low speed 30 seconds. Increase speed to medium; beat 2 minutes. Add eggs and 1 teaspoon vanilla; beat 2 minutes. Divide batter between prepared pans.

3. Bake about 20 minutes or until toothpick inserted into centers comes out clean. Cool in pans on wire rack 10 minutes. Remove from pans; cool completely on wire racks.

4. For frosting, place 1 cup cream in large bowl of electric mixer; attach whisk attachment. Whip cream at high until thickened. Add powdered sugar; whip at high speed until stiff peaks form. Transfer whipped cream to medium bowl.

5. Place cream cheese, 1 cup granulated sugar, ¼ cup butter and 1 teaspoon vanilla in mixer bowl. Beat on medium-high speed 2 to 3 minutes or until well blended and fluffy. Gently fold in whipped cream with spatula.

6. Split cake layers and place one layer on cake plate. Spread ½ cup frosting over cake; top with some of strawberries. Repeat with remaining cake and strawberries; frost top of cake with remaining frosting. Store in the refrigerator.

Apple Butter Cake

Makes 12 servings

1 cup (2 sticks) plus
   2 tablespoons butter,
   softened, divided

3 cups all-purpose flour

1½ teaspoons baking powder

1 teaspoon salt

½ teaspoon baking soda

1½ teaspoons ground
   cinnamon

¾ teaspoon ground nutmeg

½ teaspoon ground allspice
   or cloves

2¾ cups granulated sugar

4 eggs

1 cup apple butter

1 tablespoon vanilla

1 cup (8 ounces) sour cream

½ cup apple cider

Powdered sugar (optional)

1. Preheat oven to 350°F. Generously grease 10-inch tube pan with 2 tablespoons butter. Whisk flour, baking powder, salt, baking soda, cinnamon, nutmeg and allspice in medium bowl.

2. Beat remaining 1 cup butter and granulated sugar in large bowl with electric mixer at medium speed about 3 minutes or until light and fluffy. Add eggs, one at a time, beating well after each addition. Add apple butter and vanilla; beat until well blended. With mixer running on low speed, alternately add flour mixture, sour cream and cider; beat just until blended. Scrape bottom and side of bowl with spatula to bring batter together. Pour batter into prepared pan; smooth top.

3. Bake 1 hour and 10 minutes or until wooden skewer inserted near center comes out with moist crumbs. Cool in pan on wire rack 20 minutes. Place serving plate on top of pan; carefully invert cake onto plate.

4. Just before serving, if desired, place 9-inch doily over cake. Sift powdered sugar over doily; carefully remove doily.

Bananas Foster Sundae

Makes 4 servings

2 medium bananas	1½ teaspoons rum extract
¼ cup packed brown sugar	2 cups vanilla ice cream
2 tablespoons butter	Wafer cookie pieces (optional)
2 tablespoons water	

1. Peel bananas; cut into ¼-inch slices.

2. Cook brown sugar and butter in medium nonstick skillet over medium-low heat until butter is melted, stirring constantly. Stir in water; cook and stir 30 to 45 seconds or until slightly thickened. Add bananas and rum extract, stirring gently to coat in caramel mixture. Cook about 30 seconds more or until banana is heated through. Remove from heat.

3. Scoop ice cream into dessert dishes; spoon banana mixture evenly over ice cream. Garnish with wafer cookie pieces, if desired.

Dark Chocolate Coconut Cake

Makes 12 to 16 servings

Cake

- **2** cups granulated sugar
- **1½** cups all-purpose flour
- **1** cup unsweetened cocoa powder
- **2** teaspoons baking powder
- **1** teaspoon baking soda
- **1** teaspoon salt
- **1** cup buttermilk
- **3** eggs
- **6** tablespoons vegetable oil
- **1½** teaspoons vanilla
- **1** cup hot coffee*

Filling

- **½** cup evaporated milk
- **¼** cup (½ stick) butter, divided
- **3** cups mini marshmallows (or 24 large marshmallows)
- **1** package (14 ounces) shredded coconut

Ganache

- **1** cup whipping cream
- **2** cups bittersweet chocolate chips

*Or dissolve 1 teaspoon espresso powder in 1 cup boiling water.

1. Preheat oven to 350°F. Grease and flour two 8-inch cake pans.

2. Whisk sugar, flour, cocoa, baking powder, baking soda and salt in large bowl until well blended. Whisk buttermilk, eggs, oil and vanilla in medium bowl. Gradually whisk into flour mixture; whisk in coffee until smooth and well blended. Divide batter evenly between prepared pans.

3. Bake about 30 minutes or until toothpick inserted into center comes out clean. Cool in pans on wire rack 10 minutes. Remove from pans; cool completely on wire rack.

4. For filling, bring evaporated milk and 2 tablespoons butter to a boil in medium saucepan over medium heat. Add marshmallows; stir until smooth. Stir in coconut. Remove from heat; cool completely.

5. For ganache, heat cream and remaining 2 tablespoons butter in medium saucepan over medium-low heat. (Do not boil.) Remove from heat; add chocolate chips. Let stand 1 minute; stir until smooth.

6. Cut cake layers in half horizontally. Place one cake layer on serving plate; spread with one third of filling almost to edge. Repeat layers twice. Top with remaining cake layer. Frost top and side of cake with ganache; refrigerate until set. Store leftovers in refrigerator.

Peachy Keen Pies

Granny's Chocolate Meringue Pie

Makes 8 servings

½ cup granulated sugar

3 tablespoons all-purpose flour

3 tablespoons unsweetened cocoa powder

⅛ teaspoon salt

2 cups milk

3 eggs, separated

2 tablespoons butter

1 teaspoon vanilla

3 tablespoons superfine or granulated sugar

1. Grease 9-inch pie plate. Combine granulated sugar, flour, cocoa and salt in medium saucepan. Gradually whisk in milk and egg yolks; cook and stir over low heat until smooth and thickened. Remove from heat; stir in butter and vanilla. Pour into prepared pie plate; refrigerate 1 hour or until set.

2. Preheat oven to 400°F. Beat egg whites in large bowl with electric mixer at high speed until foamy. Add superfine sugar; beat until stiff peaks form. Spread meringue over pie.

3. Bake 8 to 10 minutes or until meringue is golden brown. Cool on wire rack 15 minutes.

Lemon Meringue Pie

Makes 8 servings

1 **(9-inch) deep-dish pie crust (frozen or refrigerated)**

Filling

1½ **cups water**

1 **cup sugar**

⅓ **cup cornstarch**

¼ **teaspoon salt**

4 **egg yolks**

½ **cup fresh lemon juice (3 to 4 lemons)**

2 **tablespoons grated lemon peel**

2 **tablespoons butter**

Meringue

1 **tablespoon cornstarch**

⅓ **cup water**

½ **cup sugar, divided**

½ **teaspoon vanilla**

4 **egg whites**

¼ **teaspoon cream of tartar**

1. Bake pie crust according to package directions for prebaked crust. Cool on wire rack.

2. Preheat oven to 350°F. For filling, combine 1½ cups water, 1 cup sugar, ⅓ cup cornstarch and salt in medium saucepan. Bring to a simmer over medium heat; cook and stir until mixture becomes thick and translucent. Quickly whisk in egg yolks, then add lemon juice, lemon peel and butter. Return to a simmer; cook and stir 1 minute.

3. Pour filling into medium bowl; press plastic wrap onto surface of filling. Set aside.

4. For meringue, stir 1 tablespoon cornstarch into ⅓ cup water in small saucepan until smooth. Stir in 1 tablespoon sugar and vanilla. Cook, stirring frequently, until thick paste forms. Remove from heat and cool.

5. Beat egg whites and cream of tartar in large bowl with electric mixer until foamy. Gradually add remaining sugar, beating until soft peaks form. Add cornstarch mixture, 1 tablespoon at a time, beating until stiff peaks form.

6. Spread hot filling in prepared crust. Spread meringue over filling. Bake 12 to 15 minutes or until peaks and swirls of meringue are golden brown. Cool completely before serving.

Blueberry Pie

Cream Cheese Pie Dough
(recipe follows)

2 **pints (4 cups) fresh or thawed frozen blueberries**

2 **tablespoons cornstarch**

$2/3$ **cup blueberry preserves, melted**

$1/4$ **teaspoon ground nutmeg**

1 **egg yolk**

1 **tablespoon sour cream**

1. Prepare Cream Cheese Pie Dough.

2. Preheat oven to 425°F. Roll out one disc of pastry into 11-inch circle on floured surface. Line 9-inch pie plate with pastry.

3. Combine blueberries and cornstarch in medium bowl; toss gently to coat. Stir in preserves and nutmeg. Spoon into crust.

4. Roll out remaining disc of pastry into 11-inch circle; place over fruit mixture. Turn edge under; seal and flute. Cut several slits in top crust to vent.

5. Bake 10 minutes. *Reduce oven temperature to 350°F.* Beat egg yolk and sour cream in small bowl; brush lightly over crust. Bake 40 minutes or until crust is golden brown. Cool on wire rack 15 minutes. Serve warm, cold or at room temperature.

Cream Cheese Pie Dough: Place 1½ cups flour in large bowl. Cut in ½ cup (1 stick) cold cubed butter with pastry blender or fingertips until mixture resembles coarse crumbs. Cut in 3 ounces cold cubed cream cheese and 1 teaspoon vanilla until mixture forms dough. Divide dough in half. Shape each half into a disc; wrap in plastic wrap. Refrigerate 30 minutes.

Banana Cream Pie

Makes 8 servings

1 refrigerated pie crust (half of 14-ounce package), at room temperature

²/₃ cup sugar

¼ cup cornstarch

¼ teaspoon salt

2½ cups milk

4 egg yolks, beaten

2 tablespoons butter, softened

2 teaspoons vanilla

2 medium bananas

1 teaspoon lemon juice

Whipped cream and toasted sliced almonds (optional)

1. Preheat oven to 400°F. Line 9-inch pie plate with crust; flute edge. Prick bottom and side all over with fork. Bake 10 minutes or until crust is golden brown. Cool completely on wire rack.

2. Combine sugar, cornstarch and salt in medium saucepan; whisk in milk until well blended. Cook over medium heat about 12 minutes or until mixture boils and thickens, stirring constantly. Boil 2 minutes, stirring constantly. Remove from heat.

3. Gradually whisk ½ hot cup milk mixture into egg yolks in small bowl. Gradually whisk mixture back into milk mixture in saucepan. Cook over medium heat about 5 minutes, whisking constantly. Remove from heat; whisk in butter and vanilla. Cool 20 minutes, stirring occasionally. Strain through fine-mesh strainer into medium bowl. Press plastic wrap onto surface of pudding; cool about 30 minutes or until lukewarm.

4. Cut bananas into ¼-inch slices; toss with lemon juice in medium bowl. Spread half of pudding in cooled crust; arrange bananas over pudding. (Reserve several slices for garnish, if desired.) Spread remaining pudding over bananas. Refrigerate 4 hours or overnight. Garnish with whipped cream, almonds and reserved banana slices.

Apple-Pear Praline Pie

Makes 8 servings

Double-Crust Pie Pastry (recipe follows)

4 cups sliced peeled Granny Smith apples

2 cups sliced peeled pears

3/4 cup granulated sugar

1/4 cup plus 1 tablespoon all-purpose flour, divided

4 teaspoons ground cinnamon

1/4 teaspoon salt

1/2 cup (1 stick) plus 2 tablespoons butter, divided

1 cup packed brown sugar

1 tablespoon milk

1 cup chopped pecans

1. Prepare pie pastry.

2. Combine apples, pears, granulated sugar, 1/4 cup flour, cinnamon and salt in large bowl; toss to coat. Let stand 15 minutes.

3. Preheat oven to 350°F. Roll out one disc of pastry into 11-inch circle on floured surface. Line deep-dish 9-inch pie plate with pastry; sprinkle with remaining 1 tablespoon flour. Spoon apple and pear mixture into crust; dot with 2 tablespoons butter. Roll out remaining disc of pastry into 10-inch circle. Place over fruit; seal and flute edge. Cut slits in top crust to vent.

4. Bake 1 hour. Meanwhile, combine remaining 1/2 cup butter, brown sugar and milk in small saucepan; bring to a boil over medium heat, stirring frequently. Boil 2 minutes, stirring constantly. Remove from heat; stir in pecans. Spread over pie. Cool pie on wire rack 15 minutes. Serve warm or at room temperature.

Double-Crust Pie Pastry: Combine 2 1/2 cups all-purpose flour, 1 teaspoon granulated sugar and 1 teaspoon salt in large bowl. Cut in 1 cup (2 sticks) cubed cold butter with pastry blender or fingertips until coarse crumbs form. Drizzle 1/3 cup water over flour mixture, 2 tablespoons at a time, stirring just until dough comes together. Divide dough in half. Shape each half into disc; wrap in plastic wrap. Refrigerate 30 minutes.

Strawberry Rhubarb Pie

Makes 8 servings

Double-Crust Pie Pastry (page 176)

3 cups sliced fresh or frozen rhubarb (about 1 pound)

1 pint fresh strawberries, sliced (about 3½ cups)

1 cup sugar

¼ cup cornstarch

1 teaspoon ground cinnamon

¼ teaspoon ground nutmeg

¼ teaspoon salt

1 egg yolk

1 tablespoon sour cream

1. Prepare pie pastry.

2. Combine rhubarb, strawberries, sugar, cornstarch, cinnamon, nutmeg and salt in large bowl; mix well. Let stand 30 minutes.

3. Preheat oven to 450°F. Roll out one disc of pastry into 11-inch circle on floured surface. Line deep-dish 9-inch pie plate with pastry. Trim pastry and flute edges, sealing to edge of pie plate.

4. Spoon fruit mixture into crust. Roll out remaining disc of pastry into 10-inch circle. Cut into ½-inch wide strips. Form into lattice design over fruit.

5. Whisk egg yolk and sour cream in small bowl until well blended. Brush over pastry.

6. Bake 10 minutes. *Reduce oven temperature to 350°F.* Bake 30 minutes or until pastry is golden brown and filling is hot and bubbly.* Cool on wire rack. Serve warm or at room temperature.

*Cover top loosely with foil during last 30 minutes of baking if pastry is browning too quickly.

French Silk Pie

Makes 8 servings

1 (9-inch) deep-dish pie crust (frozen or refrigerated)

1⅓ cups granulated sugar

¾ cup (1½ sticks) butter, softened

4 ounces unsweetened chocolate, melted

1½ tablespoons unsweetened cocoa powder

1 teaspoon vanilla

⅛ teaspoon salt

4 pasteurized eggs*

1 cup whipping cream

2 tablespoons powdered sugar

Chocolate curls (optional)

*The eggs in this recipe are not cooked, so use pasteurized eggs to ensure food safety.

1. Bake pie crust according to package directions. Cool completely on wire rack.

2. Beat granulated sugar and butter in large bowl with electric mixer at medium speed 4 minutes or until light and fluffy. Add melted chocolate, cocoa, vanilla and salt; beat until well blended. Add eggs, one at a time, beating 4 minutes after each addition and scraping down side of bowl occasionally.

3. Spread filling in cooled crust. Refrigerate at least 3 hours or overnight.

4. Attach whisk attachment to electric mixer. Whip cream and powdered sugar in large bowl with mixer at high speed until soft peaks form. Pipe or spread whipped cream over chocolate layer; garnish with chocolate curls.

Shoofly Pie

Makes 8 servings

1 **cup all-purpose flour**	1/2 **cup molasses**
2/3 **cup packed brown sugar**	1/2 **teaspoon baking soda**
1/4 **cup (1/2 stick) plus 1 tablespoon butter, divided**	2/3 **cup hot water**
	1 **(9-inch) deep-dish pie crust (frozen or refrigerated)**
3 **eggs**	**Whipped cream (optional)**

1. Preheat oven to 325°F. Combine flour and brown sugar in medium bowl.

2. For topping, remove 1/2 cup flour mixture to small bowl. Cut in 1 tablespoon butter with pastry blender or fingertips until mixture resembles coarse crumbs.

3. Melt remaining 1/4 cup butter in small saucepan; cool slightly. Whisk eggs, molasses and melted butter in large bowl. Gradually stir in flour mixture until well blended. Stir in baking soda. Gradually stir in hot water until blended. Pour into unbaked crust. Sprinkle with topping.

4. Bake 40 minutes or until filling is puffy and set. Cool completely on wire rack. Serve with whipped cream, if desired.

Key Lime Pie

Makes 8 servings

12 **whole graham crackers***

$^1/_3$ **cup butter, melted**

3 **tablespoons sugar**

2 **cans (14 ounces each) sweetened condensed milk**

$^3/_4$ **cup key lime juice**

6 **egg yolks**

Pinch salt

Whipped cream (optional)

Lime slices (optional)

*Or substitute 1$^1/_2$ cups graham cracker crumbs.

1. Preheat oven to 350°F. Spray 9-inch pie plate or springform pan with nonstick cooking spray.

2. Place graham crackers in food processor; pulse until coarse crumbs form. Add butter and sugar; pulse until well blended. Press mixture onto bottom and 1 inch up side of prepared pie plate. Bake 8 minutes or until lightly browned. Remove to wire rack to cool 10 minutes. *Reduce oven temperature to 325°F.*

3. Meanwhile, beat sweetened condensed milk, lime juice, egg yolks and salt in large bowl with electric mixer at medium-low speed 1 minute or until well blended and smooth. Pour into crust.

4. Bake 20 minutes or until top is set. Cool completely on wire rack. Cover; refrigerate 2 hours or overnight. Garnish with whipped cream and lime slices.

Baked Alaska Apple Butter Pie

Makes 8 servings

Single-Crust Pie Pastry (page 187)

2 cups apple butter

1 can (12 ounces) evaporated milk

3 eggs, separated

1/4 cup packed brown sugar

1 pint butter pecan ice cream, softened

1/4 teaspoon cream of tartar

1/2 teaspoon vanilla

6 tablespoons packed brown sugar

1. Prepare pie pastry. Preheat oven to 425°F. Roll out pastry into 11-inch circle on floured surface. Line 9-inch pie plate with pastry; flute edge.

2. Combine apple butter, evaporated milk, egg yolks and brown sugar in medium bowl. Pour into pie crust.

3. Bake 15 minutes. *Reduce oven temperature to 350°F.* Bake 45 minutes or until knife inserted into center comes out clean. Cool completely on wire rack. Cover and refrigerate at least 1 hour or until ready to serve.

4. Line inside of 8-inch pie plate with plastic wrap. Spread ice cream in prepared pie plate. Cover and freeze until firm.

5. Just before serving, preheat oven to 500°F. For meringue, beat egg whites and cream of tartar in large bowl with electric mixer at high speed until foamy. Beat in vanilla. Add brown sugar, 1 tablespoon at a time, beating until stiff peaks form.

6. Unmold ice cream and invert onto chilled pie. Remove plastic wrap. Spread meringue over ice cream and any exposed surface of pie, covering completely. Bake 2 to 3 minutes or until golden brown. Serve immediately.

Single-Crust Pie Pastry: Combine 1¼ cups flour and ½ teaspoon salt in medium bowl. Cut in 3 tablespoons shortening and 3 tablespoons cold cubed butter with pastry blender or fingertips until mixture resembles coarse crumbs. Combine 3 tablespoons water and ½ teaspoon cider vinegar in small bowl. Add to flour mixture; mix until dough forms, adding additional water as needed. Shape dough into disc; wrap in plastic wrap. Refrigerate 30 minutes.

Metric Conversion Chart

VOLUME MEASUREMENTS (dry)

$1/8$ teaspoon = 0.5 mL
$1/4$ teaspoon = 1 mL
$1/2$ teaspoon = 2 mL
$3/4$ teaspoon = 4 mL
1 teaspoon = 5 mL
1 tablespoon = 15 mL
2 tablespoons = 30 mL
$1/4$ cup = 60 mL
$1/3$ cup = 75 mL
$1/2$ cup = 125 mL
$2/3$ cup = 150 mL
$3/4$ cup = 175 mL
1 cup = 250 mL
2 cups = 1 pint = 500 mL
3 cups = 750 mL
4 cups = 1 quart = 1 L

VOLUME MEASUREMENTS (fluid)

1 fluid ounce (2 tablespoons) = 30 mL
4 fluid ounces ($1/2$ cup) = 125 mL
8 fluid ounces (1 cup) = 250 mL
12 fluid ounces ($1 1/2$ cups) = 375 mL
16 fluid ounces (2 cups) = 500 mL

WEIGHTS (mass)

$1/2$ ounce = 15 g
1 ounce = 30 g
3 ounces = 90 g
4 ounces = 120 g
8 ounces = 225 g
10 ounces = 285 g
12 ounces = 360 g
16 ounces = 1 pound = 450 g

DIMENSIONS

$1/16$ inch = 2 mm
$1/8$ inch = 3 mm
$1/4$ inch = 6 mm
$1/2$ inch = 1.5 cm
$3/4$ inch = 2 cm
1 inch = 2.5 cm

OVEN TEMPERATURES

250°F = 120°C
275°F = 140°C
300°F = 150°C
325°F = 160°C
350°F = 180°C
375°F = 190°C
400°F = 200°C
425°F = 220°C
450°F = 230°C

BAKING PAN SIZES

Utensil	Size in Inches/Quarts	Metric Volume	Size in Centimeters
Baking or Cake Pan (square or rectangular)	$8 \times 8 \times 2$	2 L	$20 \times 20 \times 5$
	$9 \times 9 \times 2$	2.5 L	$23 \times 23 \times 5$
	$12 \times 8 \times 2$	3 L	$30 \times 20 \times 5$
	$13 \times 9 \times 2$	3.5 L	$33 \times 23 \times 5$
Loaf Pan	$8 \times 4 \times 3$	1.5 L	$20 \times 10 \times 7$
	$9 \times 5 \times 3$	2 L	$23 \times 13 \times 7$
Round Layer Cake Pan	$8 \times 1 1/2$	1.2 L	20×4
	$9 \times 1 1/2$	1.5 L	23×4
Pie Plate	$8 \times 1 1/4$	750 mL	20×3
	$9 \times 1 1/4$	1 L	23×3
Baking Dish or Casserole	1 quart	1 L	—
	$1 1/2$ quart	1.5 L	—
	2 quart	2 L	—